Neural Computing
Theory and Practice

Neural Computing
Theory and Practice

Philip D. Wasserman

ANZA Research, Inc.

VNR | VAN NOSTRAND REINHOLD
New York

Printed in the United States of America

Van Nostrand Reinhold
115 Fifth Avenue
New York, New York 10003

Chapman & Hall
2-6 Boundary Row
London SE1 8HN, England

Thomas Nelson Australia
102 Dodds Street
South Melbourne, Victoria 3205, Australia

Nelson Canada
1120 Birchmount Road
Scarborough, Ontario M1K 5G4, Canada

16   15   14   13   12   11   10   9   8   7   6   5

Library of Congress Cataloging-in-Publication Data
Wasserman, Philip D., 1937–
    Neural computing : theory and practice / Philip D. Wasserman.
        p. cm.
    Includes bibliographies and index.
    ISBN 0-442-20743-3
    1. Neural computers.   I. Title.
    QA76.5.W353   1989   88-34842
    006.3—dc19   CIP

Contents

Preface

What are artificial neural networks? What can they do? How do they work? How can I use them? These and many similar questions are being asked by professionals from a wide variety of disciplines. Finding comprehensible answers has been difficult. University courses are few, seminars are expensive, and the literature is extensive and specialized. The several excellent books in print can prove daunting. Often expressed in technical jargon, many of the treatments assume a facility with branches of advanced mathematics that are seldom used in other specialties.

This book provides a systematic entry path for the professional who has not specialized in mathematical analysis. All of the important concepts are first expressed in ordinary English. Informal mathematical treatments are included when they clarify the explanation. Complicated derivations and proofs are placed at the end of chapters and references to other works are regularly provided. These references constitute an extensive bibliography of important writings in specific areas applicable to artificial neural networks. This multilevel approach not only provides the reader with an overview of artificial neural networks but also permits the serious student an in-depth exploration of the subject.

Every effort has been made to produce a book that is easily understood without oversimplification of the material. Readers who go on to more theoretical studies should not need to unlearn anything presented here. When simplifications are employed, they are labeled as such and references point to more detailed treatments.

This book need not be read from cover to cover. Each chapter is intended to be self-contained, assuming familiarity only with the topics of Chapters 1 and 2. While this implies a certain amount of repetition, most readers should not find it onerous.

Practicality has been a primary objective. If the chapters are studied carefully, it should be possible to implement most of the networks on a general-purpose computer. The reader is urged to do so; no other method will produce the same depth of understanding.

ACKNOWLEDGMENTS

First and foremost, I would like to thank my wife, Sarah, for her encouragement and tolerance during the months I spent in the company of my word processor.

Also, I would like to thank my friends and colleagues, who gave so generously of their time and knowledge, corrected my errors, and created an environment in which ideas developed rapidly. I would like to extend my special appreciation to Dr. Surapol Dasananda, Santa Clara University; Dr. Elizabeth Center, College of Notre Dame; Dr. Peter Rowe, College of Notre Dame; Charles Rockwell, Microlog Corp.; Tom Schwartz, The Schwartz Associates; Dennis Reinhardt, Dair Corp.; Coe Miles-Schlichting; and Douglas Marquardt. Thanks also are due to Kyla Carlson and Nang Cao for their help in preparing the illustrations.

I must, of course, take the blame for any residual errors; they couldn't watch me every minute.

Introduction

WHY ARTIFICIAL NEURAL NETWORKS?

After two decades of near eclipse, interest in artificial neural networks has grown rapidly over the past few years. Professionals from such diverse fields as engineering, philosophy, physiology, and psychology are intrigued by the potential offered by this technology and are seeking applications within their disciplines.

This resurgence of interest has been fired by both theoretical and application successes. Suddenly, it appears possible to apply computation to realms previously restricted to human intelligence; to make machines that learn and remember in ways that bear a striking resemblance to human mental processes; and to give a new and significant meaning to the much-abused term *artificial intelligence.*

CHARACTERISTICS OF ARTIFICIAL NEURAL NETWORKS

Artificial neural networks are biologically inspired; that is, they are composed of elements that perform in a manner that is analogous to the most elementary functions of the biological neuron. These elements are then organized in a way that may (or may not) be related to the anatomy of the brain. Despite this superficial resem-

1

blance, artificial neural networks exhibit a surprising number of the brain's characteristics. For example, they learn from experience, generalize from previous examples to new ones, and abstract essential characteristics from inputs containing irrelevant data.

Despite these functional similarities, not even the most optimistic advocate will suggest that artificial neural networks will soon duplicate the functions of the human brain. The actual "intelligence" exhibited by the most sophisticated artificial neural networks is below the level of a tapeworm; enthusiasm must be tempered by current reality. It is, however, equally incorrect to ignore the surprisingly brainlike performance of certain artificial neural networks. These abilities, however limited they are today, hint that a deep understanding of human intelligence may lie close at hand, and along with it a host of revolutionary applications.

Learning

Artificial neural networks can modify their behavior in response to their environment. This factor, more than any other, is responsible for the interest they have received. Shown a set of inputs (perhaps with desired outputs), they self-adjust to produce consistent responses. A wide variety of training algorithms has been developed, each with its own strengths and weaknesses. As we point out later in this volume, there are important questions yet to be answered regarding what things a network can be trained to do, and how the training should be performed.

Generalization

Once trained, a network's response can be, to a degree, insensitive to minor variations in its input. This ability to see through noise and distortion to the pattern that lies within is vital to pattern recognition in a real-world environment. Overcoming the literal-mindedness of the conventional computer, it produces a system that can deal with the imperfect world in which we live. It is important to note that the artificial neural network generalizes automatically as a result of its structure, not by using human intelligence embedded in the form of ad hoc computer programs.

Abstraction

Some artificial neural networks are capable of abstracting the essence of a set of inputs. For example, a network can be trained on a sequence of distorted versions of the letter A. After adequate training, application of such a distorted example will cause the network to produce a perfectly formed letter. In one sense, it has learned to produce something that it has never seen before.

This ability to extract an ideal from imperfect inputs raises interesting philosophical issues; it is reminiscent of the concept of ideals found in Plato's *Republic*. In any case, extracting idealized prototypes is a highly useful ability in humans; it seems that now we may share it with artificial neural networks.

Applicability

Artificial neural networks are not a panacea. They are clearly unsuited to such tasks as calculating the payroll. It appears that they will, however, become the preferred technique for a large class of pattern-recognition tasks that conventional computers do poorly, if at all.

HISTORICAL PERSPECTIVE

Humans have always wondered about their own thoughts. This self-referential inquiry, the mind thinking of itself, may be a uniquely human characteristic. Speculations on the nature of thought abound, ranging from the spiritual to the anatomical. With philosophers and theologians often opposing the opinions of physiologists and anatomists, the questions have been hotly debated to little avail, as the subject is notoriously difficult to study. Those relying on introspection and speculation have arrived at conclusions that lack the rigor demanded by the physical sciences. Experimenters have found the brain and nervous system to be difficult to observe and perplexing in organization. In short, the powerful methods of scientific inquiry that have changed our view of physical reality have been slow in finding application to the understanding of humans themselves.

Neurobiologists and neuroanatomists have made substantial progress. Painstakingly mapping out the structure and function of the human nervous system, they came to understand much of the brain's "wiring," but little of its operation. As their knowledge grew, the complexity was found to be staggering. Hundreds of billions of neurons, each connecting to hundreds or thousands of others, comprise a system that dwarfs our most ambitious dreams of supercomputers. Nevertheless, the brain is gradually yielding its secrets to one of humankind's most sustained and ambitious inquiries.

The improved understanding of the functioning of the neuron and the pattern of its interconnections has allowed researchers to produce mathematical models to test their theories. Experiments can now be conducted on digital computers without involving human or animal subjects, thereby solving many practical and ethical problems. From early work it became apparent that these models not only mimicked functions of the brain, but that they were capable of performing useful functions in their own right. Hence, two mutually reinforcing objectives of neural modeling were defined and remain today: first, to understand the physiological and psychological functioning of the human neural system; and second, to produce computational systems (artificial neural networks) that perform brainlike functions. It is the latter objective that is the major focus of this book.

Along with the progress in neuroanatomy and neurophysiology, psychologists were developing models of human learning. One such model, which has proved most fruitful, was that of D. O. Hebb, who in 1949 proposed a learning law that became the starting point for artificial neural network training algorithms. Augmented today by many other methods, it showed scientists of that era how a network of neurons could exhibit learning behavior.

In the 1950s and 1960s, a group of researchers combined these biological and psychological insights to produce the first artificial neural networks. Initially implemented as electronic circuits, they were later converted to the more flexible medium of computer simulation, the most common realization today. Early successes produced a burst of activity and optimism. Marvin Minsky, Frank Rosenblatt, Bernard Widrow, and others developed networks consisting of a single layer of artificial neurons. Often called perceptrons, they were applied to such diverse problems as weather prediction, electrocardiogram analysis, and artificial vision. It seemed for a time that the key to intelligence had been found; reproducing the human brain was only a matter of constructing a large enough network.

This illusion was soon dispelled. Networks failed to solve problems superficially similar to those they had been successful in solving. These unexplained failures launched a period of intense analysis. Marvin Minsky, carefully applying mathematical techniques, developed rigorous theorems regarding network operation. His research led to the publication of the book *Perceptrons* (Minsky and Papert 1969), in which he and Seymore Papert proved that the single-layer networks then in use were theoretically incapable of solving many simple problems, including the function performed by a simple exclusive-or gate. Nor was Minsky optimistic about the potential for progress:

> The Perceptron has shown itself worthy of study despite (and even because of!) its severe limitations. It has many features that attract attention: its linearity; its intriguing learning theorem; its clear paradigmatic simplicity as a kind of parallel computation. There is no reason to suppose that any of these virtues carry over to the many-layered version. Nevertheless, we consider it to be an important research problem to elucidate (or reject) our intuitive judgment that the extension is sterile.
>
> Perhaps some powerful convergence theorem will be discovered, or some profound reason for the failure to produce an interesting "learning theorem" for the multilayered machine will be found. (pp. 231–32)

Minsky's brilliance, rigor, and prestige gave the book great credibility: its conclusions were unassailable. Discouraged researchers left the field for areas of greater promise, government agencies redirected their funding, and artificial neural networks lapsed into obscurity for nearly two decades.

Nevertheless, a few dedicated scientists such as Teuvo Kohonen, Stephen Grossberg, and James Anderson continued their efforts. Often underfunded and unappreciated, some researchers had difficulty finding publishers; hence, research published during the

1970s and early 1980s is found scattered among a wide variety of journals, some of which are rather obscure. Gradually, a theoretical foundation emerged, upon which the more powerful multilayer networks of today are being constructed. Minsky's appraisal has proven excessively pessimistic; networks are now routinely solving many of the problems that he posed in his book.

In the past few years, theory has been translated into application, and new corporations dedicated to the commercialization of the technology have appeared. There has been an explosive increase in the amount of research activity. With four major conventions in 1987 in the field of artificial neural networks, and over 500 technical papers published, the growth rate has been phenomenal.

The lesson to be learned from this history is found in Clark's law. Propounded by the writer and scientist Arthur C. Clark, it states in effect that if a respected senior scientist says a thing can be done, he or she is almost always correct; if the scientist says it cannot be done, he or she is almost always wrong. The history of science is a chronicle of mistakes and partial truths. Today's dogma becomes tomorrow's rubbish. Unquestioning acceptance of "facts," whatever the source, can cripple scientific inquiry. From one point of view, Minsky's excellent scientific work led to an unfortunate hiatus in the progress of artificial neural networks. There is no doubt, however, that the field had been plagued by unsupported optimism and an inadequate theoretical basis. It may be that the shock provided by *Perceptrons* allowed a period for the necessary maturation of the field.

ARTIFICIAL NEURAL NETWORKS TODAY

There have been many impressive demonstrations of artificial neural network capabilities: a network has been trained to convert text to phonetic representations, which were then converted to speech by other means (Sejnowsky and Rosenberg 1987); another network can recognize handwritten characters (Burr 1987); and a neural network–based image-compression system has been devised (Cottrell, Munro, and Zipser 1987). These all use the backpropagation network, perhaps the most successful of the current algorithms. Backpropagation, invented independently in three separate research efforts (Werbos 1974; Parker 1982; and Rumelhart, Hinton, and Williams 1986), provides a systematic means for training multilayer networks, thereby overcoming limitations presented by Minsky.

As we point out in the chapters that follow, backpropagation is not without its problems. First, there is no guarantee that the network can be trained in a finite amount of time. Many training efforts fail after consuming large amounts of computer time. When this happens, the training attempt must be repeated—with no certainty that the results will be any better. Also, there is no assurance that the network will train to the best configuration possible. So-called local minima can trap the training algorithm in an inferior solution.

Many other network algorithms have been developed that have specific advantages; several of these are discussed in the chapters that follow. It should be emphasized that none of today's networks represents a panacea; all of them suffer from limitations in their ability to learn and recall.

We are presented with a field having demonstrated performance, unique potential, many limitations, and a host of unanswered questions. It is a situation calling for optimism tempered with caution. Authors tend to publish their successes and give their failures little publicity, thereby creating an impression that may not be realistic. Those seeking venture capital to start new firms must present a convincing projection of substantial accomplishments and profits. There exists, therefore, a substantial danger that artificial neural networks will be oversold before their time, promising performance without the capability for delivery. If this happens, the entire field could suffer a loss of credibility, possibly relapsing into the Dark Ages of the 1970s. Much solid work is required to improve existing networks. New techniques must be developed, existing methods strengthened, and the theoretical foundation broadened before this field can realize its full potential.

PROSPECTS FOR THE FUTURE

Artificial neural networks have been proposed for tasks ranging from battlefield management to minding the baby. Potential applications are those where human intelligence functions effortlessly and conventional computation has proven cumbersome or inadequate. This application class is at least as large as that serviced by conventional computation, and the vision arises of artificial neural networks taking their place alongside of conventional computation as an adjunct of equal size and importance. This will happen only if fundamental research yields results at a rapid rate, as today's theoretical foundations are inadequate to support such projections.

Artificial Neural Networks and Expert Systems

The field of artificial intelligence has been dominated in recent years by the logical- and symbol-manipulation disciplines. For example, expert systems have been widely acclaimed and have achieved many notable successes—as well as many failures. Some say that artificial neural networks will replace current artificial intelligence, but there are many indications that the two will coexist and be combined into systems in which each technique performs the tasks for which it is best suited.

This viewpoint is supported by the way that humans operate in the world. Activities requiring rapid responses are governed by pattern recognition. Since actions are produced rapidly and without conscious effort, this mode of operation is essential for the quick, spontaneous responses needed to survive in a hostile environment. Consider the consequences if our ancestors had to reason out the correct response to a leaping carnivore!

When our pattern-recognition system fails to produce an unambiguous interpretation (and when time permits), the matter is referred to the higher mental functions. These may require more information and certainly more time, but the quality of the resulting decisions can be superior.

One can envision an artificial system that mimics this division of labor. An artificial neural network would produce an appropriate response to its environment under most circumstances. Because such networks can indicate the confidence level associated with each decision, it would ''know that it did not know,'' and would refer that case to an expert system for resolution. The decisions made at this higher level would be concrete and logical, but might require the gathering of additional facts before a conclusion could be reached. The combination of the two systems would be more robust than either acting alone, and it would follow the highly successful model provided by biological evolution.

Reliability Considerations

Before artificial neural networks can be applied where human life or valuable assets are at stake, questions regarding their reliability must be resolved.

Like the humans whose brain structure they mimic, artificial neural networks retain a degree of unpredictability. Unless every possible input is tried, there is no way to be certain of the precise output. In a large network such exhaustive testing is impractical and statistical estimates of performance must suffice. Under some circumstances this is intolerable. For example, what is an acceptable error rate for a network controlling a space defense system? Most people would say that any error is intolerable; it might result in unthinkable death and destruction. This attitude is not changed by the fact that a human in the same situation might also make mistakes.

The problem lies in the expectation that computers are absolutely error free. Because artificial neural networks will sometimes make errors even when they are functioning correctly, many feel that this translates into unreliability, a characteristic we have found unacceptable in our machines.

A related difficulty lies in the inability of traditional artificial neural networks to "explain" how they solve problems. The internal representations that result from training are often so complex as to defy analysis in all but the most trivial cases. This is closely related to our inability to explain how we recognize a person despite differences in distance, angle, illumination, and the passage of years. An expert system can trace back through its own reasoning process so that a human can check it for reasonableness. Incorporation of this ability into artificial neural networks has been reported (Gallant 1988) and its development may have an important effect upon the acceptability of these systems.

SUMMARY

Artificial neural networks represent a major extension of computation. They promise human-made devices that perform functions heretofore reserved for human beings. Dull, repetitive, or dangerous tasks can be performed by machines and entirely new applications will arise as the technology matures.

The theoretical foundations of artificial neural networks are expanding rapidly, but they are currently inadequate to support the more optimistic projections. Viewed historically, theory has developed faster than pessimists had projected and slower than optimists had hoped, a typical situation. Today's surge of interest has set thousands of researchers to work in the field. It is reasonable to expect a rapid increase in our understanding of artificial neural networks leading to improved network paradigms and a host of application opportunities.

References

Burr, D. J. 1987. Experiments with a connectionist text reader. In *Proceedings of the First International Conference on Neural Networks,* eds. M. Caudill and C. Butler, vol. 4, pp. 717–24. San Diego, CA: SOS Printing.

Cottrell, G. W., Munro, P., and Zipser, D. 1987. Image compression by backpropagation: An example of extensional programming. *Advances in cognitive science* (vol. 3). Norwood, NJ: Ablex.

Gallant, S. I. 1988. Connectionist expert systems. *Communications of the ACM* 31:152–69.

Minsky, M., and Papert, S. 1969. *Perceptrons.* Cambridge, MA: MIT Press.

Parker, D. B. 1982. Learning-logic. Invention Report, S81-64, File 1. Office of Technology Licensing, Stanford University.

Rumelhart, D. E., Hinton, G. E., and Williams, R. J. 1986. Learning internal representations by error propagation. In *Parallel distributed processing*, vol. 1, pp. 318–62. Cambridge, MA: MIT Press.

Sejnowski, T. J., and Rosenberg, C. R. 1987. Parallel networks that learn to pronounce English text. *Complex Systems* 3:145–68.

Werbos, P. J. 1974. *Beyond regression: New tools for prediction and analysis in the behavioral sciences.* Masters thesis, Harvard University.

1

Fundamentals of Artificial Neural Networks

Artificial neural networks have been developed in a wide variety of configurations. Despite this apparent diversity, network paradigms have a great deal in common. In this chapter, recurring themes are briefly identified and discussed so they will be familiar when encountered later in the book.

Notation and representations presented here have been selected as most representative of current practice (there are no published standards), and are used throughout the book.

THE BIOLOGICAL PROTOTYPE

Artificial neural networks are biologically inspired; that is, researchers are usually thinking about the organization of the brain when considering network configurations and algorithms. At this point the correspondence may end. Knowledge about the brain's overall operation is so limited that there is little to guide those who would emulate it. Hence, network designers must go beyond current biological knowledge, seeking structures that perform useful functions. In many cases, this necessary shift discards biological plausibility; the brain becomes a metaphor; networks are produced that are organically infeasible or require a highly improbable set of assumptions about brain anatomy and functioning.

Despite this tenuous, often nonexistent relationship with biology, artificial neural networks continue to evoke comparisons with the brain. Their functions are often reminiscent of human cognition; hence, it is difficult to avoid making the analogy. Unfortunately, such comparisons are not benign; they create unrealistic expectations that inevitably result in disillusionment. Research funding based on false hopes can evaporate in the harsh light of reality as it did in the 1960s, and this promising field could again go into eclipse if restraint is not exercised.

Despite the preceding caveats, it remains profitable to understand something of the mammalian nervous system; it is an entity that successfully performs the tasks to which our artificial systems only aspire. The following discussion is brief; Appendix A provides a more extensive (but by no means complete) treatment of the mammalian nervous system for those who wish to know more about this fascinating subject.

The human nervous system, built of cells called neurons, is of staggering complexity. An estimated 10^{11} neurons participate in perhaps 10^{15} interconnections over transmission paths that may range for a meter or more. Each neuron shares many characteristics with the other cells in the body, but has unique capabilities to receive, process, and transmit electrochemical signals over the neural pathways that comprise the brain's communication system.

Figure 1-1 shows the structure of a pair of typical biological neurons. Dendrites extend from the cell body to other neurons where they receive signals at a connection point called a synapse. On the receiving side of the synapse, these inputs are conducted to the cell body. There they are summed, some inputs tending to excite the cell, others tending to inhibit its firing. When the cumulative excitation in the cell body exceeds a threshold, the cell fires, sending a signal down the axon to other neurons. This basic functional outline has many complexities and exceptions; nevertheless, most artificial neural networks model only these simple characteristics.

THE ARTIFICIAL NEURON

The artificial neuron was designed to mimic the first-order characteristics of the biological neuron. In essence, a set of inputs are

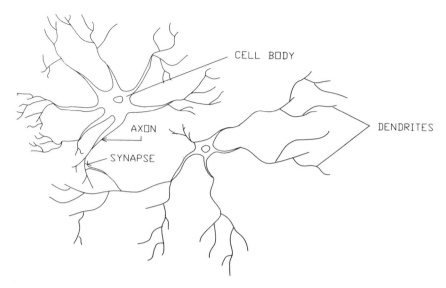

CELL BODY

AXON

SYNAPSE

DENDRITES

Figure 1-1. Biological Neuron

applied, each representing the output of another neuron. Each input is multiplied by a corresponding weight, analogous to a synaptic strength, and all of the weighted inputs are then summed to determine the activation level of the neuron. Figure 1-2 shows a model that implements this idea. Despite the diversity of network paradigms, nearly all are based upon this configuration. Here, a set of inputs labeled $x_1, x_2, \ldots, x_n$ is applied to the artificial neuron. These inputs, collectively referred to as the vector* **X**, correspond to the signals into the synapses of a biological neuron. Each signal is multiplied by an associated weight $w_1, w_2, \ldots, w_n$, before it is applied to the summation block, labeled Σ. Each weight corresponds to the "strength" of a single biological synaptic connection. (The set of weights is referred to collectively as the vector **W**.) The summation block, corresponding roughly to the biologi-

---

*A few forms of vector notation are used throughout the book. Doing so dramatically simplifies mathematical expressions, thereby preventing the details from obscuring the concepts. Appendix B contains a short tutorial on the vector notation that is used. If your vector skills are rusty, reading this short tutorial now will bring great rewards in speed and depth of comprehension of the material that follows.

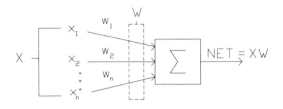

$$\text{NET} = x_1\,w_1 + x_2\,w_2 + \;...\; + x_n\,w_n$$

Figure 1-2.   Artificial Neuron

cal cell body, adds all of the weighted inputs algebraically, producing an output that we call NET. This may be compactly stated in vector notation as follows:

$$\text{NET} = \mathbf{XW}$$

Activation Functions

The NET signal is usually further processed by an activation function F to produce the neuron's output signal, *OUT*. This may be a simple linear function,

$$\text{OUT} = K(\text{NET})$$

where K is a constant, a threshold function,

$$\text{OUT} = 1 \quad \text{if NET} > T$$
$$\text{OUT} = 0 \quad \text{otherwise}$$

where T is a constant threshold value, or a function that more accurately simulates the nonlinear transfer characteristic of the biological neuron and permits more general network functions.

In Figure 1-3 the block labeled F accepts the NET output and produces the signal labeled OUT. If the F processing block compresses the range of NET, so that OUT never exceeds some low limits regardless of the value of NET, *F* is called a *squashing function*. The squashing function is often chosen to be the logistic function or "sigmoid" (meaning S-shaped) as shown in Figure 1-4a. This function is expressed mathematically as $F(x) = 1/(1 + e^{-x})$. Thus,

$$OUT = 1/(1 + e^{-NET})$$

By analogy to analog electronic systems, we may think of the activation function as defining a nonlinear gain for the artificial neuron. This gain is calculated by finding the ratio of the change in OUT to a small change in NET. Thus, gain is the slope of the curve at a specific excitation level. It varies from a low value at large negative excitations (the curve is nearly horizontal), to a high value at zero excitation, and it drops back as excitation becomes very large and positive. Grossberg (1973) found that this nonlinear gain characteristic solves the noise-saturation dilemma that he posed; that is, how can the same network handle both small and large signals? Small input signals require high gain through the network if they are to produce usable output; however, a large number of cascaded high-gain stages can saturate the output with the amplified noise (random variations) that is present in any realizable network. Also, large input signals will saturate high-gain stages, again eliminating any usable output. The central high-gain region of the logistic function solves the problem of processing small signals, while its regions of decreasing gain at positive and negative extremes are appropriate for large excitations. In this way, a neuron performs with appropriate gain over a wide range of input levels.

Another commonly used activation function is the hyperbolic

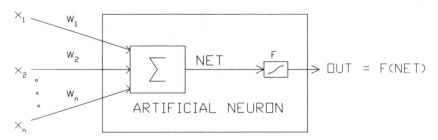

Figure 1-3.   Artificial Neuron with Activation Function

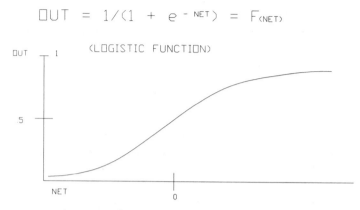

$$OUT = 1/(1 + e^{-NET}) = F_{(NET)}$$

Figure 1-4a.   Sigmoidal Logistic Function

tangent. It is similar in shape to the logistic function and is often used by biologists as a mathematical model of nerve-cell activation. Used as an artificial neural network activation function it is expressed as follows:

$$OUT = \tanh(x)$$

Like the logistic function, the hyperbolic tangent function is S shaped, but is symmetrical about the origin, resulting in OUT having the value 0 when NET is 0 (see Figure 1-4b). Unlike the logistic function, the hyperbolic tangent function has a bipolar value for OUT, a characteristic that has been shown to be beneficial in certain networks (see Chapter 3).

This simple model of the artificial neuron ignores many of the characteristics of its biological counterpart. For example, it does not take into account time delays that affect the dynamics of the system; inputs produce an immediate output. More important, it does not include the effects of synchronism or the frequency-modulation function of the biological neuron, characteristics that some researchers feel to be crucial.

Despite these limitations, networks formed of these neurons exhibit attributes that are strongly reminiscent of the biological system. Perhaps enough of the essential nature of the biological neuron has been captured to produce responses like the biological system, or perhaps the similarity is coincidental; only time and research will tell.

SINGLE-LAYER ARTIFICIAL NEURAL NETWORKS

Although a single neuron can perform certain simple pattern detection functions, the power of neural computation comes from connecting neurons into networks. The simplest network is a group of neurons arranged in a layer as shown on the right side of Figure 1-5. Note that the circular nodes on the left serve only to distribute the inputs; they perform no computation and hence will not be considered to constitute a layer. For this reason, they are shown as circles to distinguish them from the computing neurons, which are shown as squares. The set of inputs **X** has each of its elements connected to each artificial neuron through a separate weight. Early artificial neural networks were no more complex than this. Each neuron simply output a weighted sum of the inputs to the network. Actual artificial and biological networks may have many of the connections deleted, but full connectivity is shown

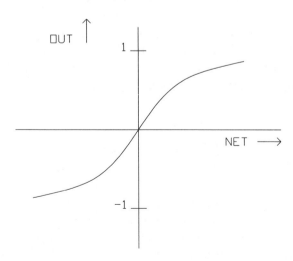

Figure 1-4b. Hyperbolic Tangent Function

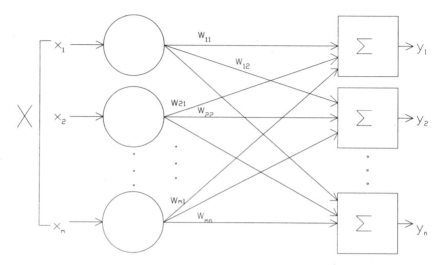

Figure 1-5.   Single-Layer Neural Network

for reasons of generality. Also, there may be connections between the outputs and inputs of neurons in a layer; such configurations are treated in Chapter 6.

It is convenient to consider the weights to be elements of a matrix **W**. The dimensions of the matrix are m rows by n columns, where m is the number of inputs and n the number of neurons. For example, the weight connecting the third input to the second neuron would be $w_{3,2}$. In this way it may be seen that calculating the set of neuron NET outputs **N** for a layer is a simple matrix multiplication. Thus $N = XW$, where **N** and **X** are row vectors.

MULTILAYER ARTIFICIAL NEURAL NETWORKS

Larger, more complex networks generally offer greater computational capabilities. Although networks have been constructed in every imaginable configuration, arranging neurons in layers mimics the layered structure of certain portions of the brain. These multilayer networks have been proven to have capabilities beyond those of a single layer (see Chapter 2), and in recent years, algorithms have been developed to train them.

Multilayer networks may be formed by simply cascading a group of single layers; the output of one layer provides the input to the subsequent layer. Figure 1-6 shows such a network, again drawn fully connected.

The Nonlinear Activation Function

Multilayer networks provide no increase in computational power over a single-layer network unless there is a nonlinear activation function between layers. Calculating the output of a layer consists of multiplying the input vector by the first weight matrix, and then (if there is no nonlinear activation function) multiplying the resulting vector by the second weight matrix. This may be expressed as:

$$(\mathbf{X}\mathbf{W}_1)\mathbf{W}_2$$

Since matrix multiplication is associative, the terms may be regrouped and written:

$$\mathbf{X}(\mathbf{W}_1\mathbf{W}_2)$$

This shows that a two-layer linear network is exactly equivalent to a single layer having a weight matrix equal to the product of the two weight matrixes. Hence, any multilayer linear network can be replaced by an equivalent one-layer network. In Chapter 2 we point out that single-layer networks are severely limited in their computational capability; thus, the nonlinear activation functions are vital to the expansion of the network's capability beyond that of the single-layer network.

Recurrent Networks

The networks considered up to this point have no feedback connections, that is, connections through weights extending from the outputs of a layer to the inputs of the same or previous layers. This

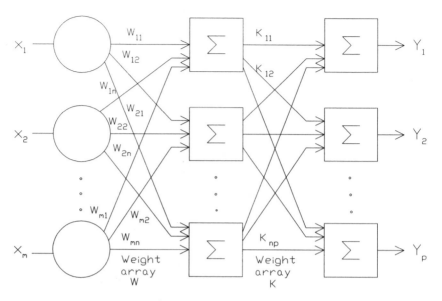

Figure 1-6.   Two-Layer Neural Network

special class, called nonrecurrent or feedforward networks, is of considerable interest and is widely applied.

More general networks that do contain feedback connections are said to be recurrent. Nonrecurrent networks have no memory; their output is solely determined by the current inputs and the values of the weights. In some configurations, recurrent networks recirculate previous outputs back to inputs; hence, their output is determined both by their current input and their previous outputs. For this reason recurrent networks can exhibit properties very similar to short-term memory in humans in that the state of the network outputs depends in part upon their previous inputs.

TERMINOLOGY, NOTATION, AND REPRESENTATION OF ARTIFICIAL NEURAL NETWORKS

Unfortunately, there are neither published standards nor general agreement among authors regarding terms, notation, and the graphical representations for artificial neural networks. Identical network paradigms can appear entirely differently when presented by different authors. In this book, the most common and self-descriptive terms have been selected and used consistently.

Terminology

Many authors avoid the term "neuron" when referring to the artificial neuron, recognizing that it is a crude approximation of its biological model. This book uses the terms "neuron," "cell," and "unit" interchangeably as shorthand for "artificial neuron," as these words are succinct and self-explanatory.

Notation: Differential Equations versus Difference Equations

Learning algorithms, like artificial neural networks in general, can be presented in either differential-equation or difference-equation form. The differential-equation representation assumes that the processes are continuous, operating much like a large analog network. Viewing the biological system at a microscopic level, this is not true; the activation level of a biological neuron is determined by the average rate at which it emits discrete action potential pulses down its axon. This average rate is commonly treated as an analog quantity, but it is important to remember the underlying reality.

If one wishes to simulate artificial neural networks on an analog computer, differential-equation representations are highly desirable. However, most work today is being done on digital computers, making the difference-equation form most appropriate, as these equations can be converted easily into computer programs. For this reason, the difference-equation representation is used throughout this volume.

Representation

The literature shows little agreement about the way to count the number of layers in a network. Figure 1-6 shows that a multilayer network consists of alternating sets of neurons and weights. As previously discussed in connection with Figure 1-5, the input layer does no summation; these neurons serve only as fan-out points to the first set of weights and do not affect the computational capability of the network. For this reason, the first layer is not included in the layer count and a network such as that shown in Figure 1-6 is referred to as a two-layer network, as only two layers are performing the computation. Also, the weights of a layer are assumed to be associated with the neurons that follow them. Therefore, a layer consists of a set of weights and the subsequent neurons that sum the signals they carry.

TRAINING OF ARTIFICIAL NEURAL NETWORKS

Of all of the interesting characteristics of artificial neural networks, none captures the imagination like their ability to learn. Their training shows so many parallels to the intellectual development of human beings that it may seem that we have achieved a fundamental understanding of this process. The euphoria should be tempered with caution; learning in artificial neural networks is limited, and many difficult problems remain to be solved before it can be determined if we are even on the right track. Nevertheless, impressive demonstrations have been performed, such as Sejnowski's NetTalk (see Chapter 3), and many other practical applications are emerging.

Objective of Training

A network is trained so that application of a set of inputs produces the desired (or at least consistent) set of outputs. Each such input (or output) set is referred to as a vector. Training is accomplished by sequentially applying input vectors, while adjusting network weights according to a predetermined procedure. During training, the network weights gradually converge to values such that each input vector produces the desired output vector.

Supervised Training

Training algorithms are categorized as supervised and unsupervised. Supervised training requires the pairing of each input vector with a target vector representing the desired output; together these are called a *training pair*. Usually a network is trained over a number of such training pairs. An input vector is applied, the output of the network is calculated and compared to the corresponding target vector, and the difference (error) is fed back through the network and weights are changed according to an algorithm that tends to minimize the error. The vectors of the training set are applied sequentially, and errors are calculated and weights adjusted for each vector, until the error for the entire training set is at an acceptably low level.

Unsupervised Training

Despite many application successes, supervised training has been criticized as being biologically implausible; it is difficult to conceive of a training mechanism in the brain that compares desired and actual outputs, feeding processed corrections back through the network. If this were the brain's mechanism, where do the desired output patterns come from? How could the brain of an infant accomplish the self-organization that has been proven to exist in early development? Unsupervised training is a far more plausible model of learning in the biological system. Developed by Kohonen (1984) and many others, it requires no target vector for the outputs, and hence, no comparisons to predetermined ideal responses. The training set consists solely of input vectors. The training algorithm modifies network weights to produce output vectors that are consistent; that is, both application of one of the training vectors or application of a vector that is sufficiently similar to it will produce the same pattern of outputs. The training process, therefore, extracts the statistical properties of the training set and groups similar vectors into classes. Applying a vector from a given class to the input will produce a specific output vector, but there is no way to determine prior to training which specific output pattern will be produced by a given input vector class. Hence, the outputs of such a network must generally be transformed into a comprehensible form subsequent to the training process. This does not represent a serious problem. It is usually a simple matter to identify the input–output relationships established by the network.

Training Algorithms

Most of today's training algorithms have evolved from the concepts of D. O. Hebb (1961). He proposed a model for unsupervised learning in which the synaptic strength (weight) was increased if both the source and destination neuron were activated. In this way, often-used paths in the network are strengthened, and the phenomena of habit and learning through repetition are explained.

An artificial neural network using Hebbian learning will increase its network weights according to the product of the excitation levels of the source and destination neurons. In symbols:

$$w_{ij}(n + 1) = w_{ij}(n) + \alpha \, \text{OUT}_i \text{OUT}_j$$

where

$w_{ij}(n)$ = the value of a weight from neuron i to neuron j prior to adjustment

$w_{ij}(n + 1)$ = the value of a weight from neuron i to neuron j after adjustment

α = the learning-rate coefficient

OUT_i = the output of neuron i and input to neuron j

OUT_j = the output of neuron j

Networks have been constructed that use Hebbian learning; however, more effective training algorithms have been developed over the past 20 years. In particular the work of Rosenblatt (1962), Widrow (1959), Widrow and Hoff (1960), and many others developed supervised learning algorithms, producing networks that learned a broader range of input patterns, and at higher learning rates, than could be accomplished using simple Hebbian learning.

There are a tremendous variety of training algorithms in use today; a book larger than this one would be required to give this topic a complete treatment. To deal with this diverse subject in an organized if not exhaustive fashion, each of the chapters that follow presents the detailed training algorithms for the paradigm under consideration. In addition, Appendix C gives a general overview that is somewhat wider though not as deep. It presents the historical context of training methods, their general taxonomy, and certain of their advantages and limitations. This will, of necessity, repeat some of the material from the text, but the broadened perspective should justify the repetition.

PROLOGUE

In the chapters that follow some of the most important network configurations and their training algorithms are presented and analyzed. These paradigms represent a cross section of the art, both past and present. If carefully studied, many other paradigms will be seen to be easily understood modifications. New developments are generally evolutionary rather than revolutionary, so understanding the paradigms in this book will enhance one's ability to follow the progress of this rapidly moving field.

The emphasis of the presentation is intuitive and algorithmic rather than mathematical. It is more inclined toward the user of artificial neural networks rather than toward the theorist; therefore, enough information is given to allow the reader to understand the fundamental ideas. Also, one who knows computer programming should be able to implement each of the networks. Detailed derivations and complicated mathematics have been omitted unless they bear directly upon network implementation. For the more analytical reader, references are provided to books and papers that are more rigorous and complete.

References

Grossberg, S. 1973. Contour enhancement, short-term memory, and consistencies in reverberating neural networks. *Studies in Applied Mathematics* 52:217, 257.

Hebb, D. O. 1961. *Organization of behavior*. New York: Science Editions.

Kohonen, T. 1984. *Self-organization and associative memory*. Series in Information Sciences, vol. 8. Berlin: Springer Verlag.

Rosenblatt, F. 1962. *Principles of neurodynamics*. New York: Spartan Books.

Widrow, B. 1959. Adaptive sampled-data systems, a statistical theory of adaptation. *1959 IRE WESCON Convention Record*, part 4, pp. 88–91. New York: Institute of Radio Engineers.

Widrow, B., and Hoff, M. 1960. Adaptive switching circuits. *1960 IRE WESCON Convention Record*, pp. 96–104. New York: Institute of Radio Engineers.

2

Perceptrons

PERCEPTRONS AND THE EARLY DAYS OF ARTIFICIAL NEURAL NETWORKS

The science of artificial neural networks made its first significant appearance in the 1940s. Researchers desiring to duplicate the functions of the human brain developed simple hardware (and later software) models of the biological neuron and its interconnection system. As the neurophysiologists gradually gained an improved understanding of the human neural system, these early attempts were seen to be gross approximations. Still, impressive results were achieved that encouraged further research and resulted in networks of greater sophistication.

McCulloch and Pitts (1943) published the first systematic study of artificial neural networks. In later work (Pitts and McCulloch 1947), they explored network paradigms for pattern recognition despite translation and rotation. Much of their work involved the simple neuron model shown in Figure 2-1. The Σ unit multiplies each input x by a weight w, and sums the weighted inputs. If this sum is greater than a predetermined threshold, the output is one; otherwise it is zero. These systems (and their many variations) collectively have been called *perceptrons*. In general, they consist of a single layer of artificial neurons connected by weights to a set of inputs (see Figure 2-2), although more complicated networks bear the same name.

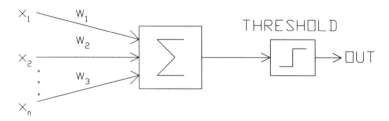

Figure 2-1.   Perceptron Neuron

In the 1960s, perceptrons created a great deal of interest and optimism. Rosenblatt (1962) proved a remarkable theorem about perceptron learning (explained below). Widrow (Widrow 1961, 1963; Widrow and Angell 1962; Widrow and Hoff 1960) made a number of convincing demonstrations of perceptron-like systems, and researchers throughout the world were eagerly exploring the potential of these systems. The initial euphoria was replaced by disillusionment as perceptrons were found to fail at certain simple learning tasks. Minsky (Minsky and Papert 1969) analyzed this problem with great rigor and proved that there are severe restrictions on what a single-layer perceptron can represent, and hence, on what it can learn. Because there were no techniques known at that time for training multilayer networks, researchers turned to

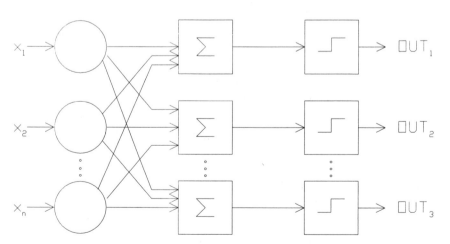

Figure 2-2.   Multioutput Perceptron

more promising areas, and artificial neural network research went into near eclipse. The recent discovery of training methods for multilayer networks has, more than any other factor, been responsible for the resurgence of interest and research effort.

Minsky's work may have dampened the ardor of the perceptron enthusiasts, but it provided a period for needed consolidation and development of the underlying theory. It is important to note that Minsky's analysis has not been refuted; it remains an important work and must be studied if the errors of the 1960s are not to be repeated.

Despite the limitations of perceptrons, they have been extensively studied (if not widely used). Their theory is the foundation for many other forms of artificial neural networks and they demonstrate important principles. For these reasons, they are a logical starting point for a study of artificial neural networks.

PERCEPTRON REPRESENTATION

The proof of the perceptron learning theorem (Rosenblatt 1962) demonstrated that a perceptron could learn anything it could represent. It is important to distinguish between representation and learning. Representation refers to the ability of a perceptron (or other network) to simulate a specified function. Learning requires the existence of a systematic procedure for adjusting the network weights to produce that function.

To illustrate the representation problem, suppose we have a set of flash cards bearing the numerals 0 through 9. Suppose also that we have a hypothetical machine that is capable of distinguishing the odd-numbered cards from the even-numbered ones, lighting an indicator on its panel when shown an odd-numbered card (see Figure 2-3). Can such a machine be represented by a perceptron? That is, can a perceptron be constructed and its weights adjusted (regardless of how it is done) so that it has the same discriminatory capability? If so, we say that the perceptron can represent the desired machine. We shall see that the single-layer perceptron is seriously limited in its representational ability; there are many simple machines that the perceptron cannot represent no matter how the weights are adjusted.

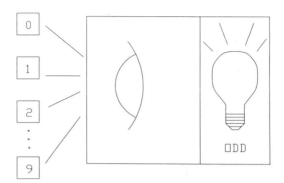

Figure 2-3.   Image-Recognition System

Exclusive-Or Problem

One of Minsky's more discouraging results shows that a single-layer perceptron cannot simulate a simple exclusive-or function. This function accepts two inputs that can be only zero or one. It produces an output of one only if either input is one (but not both). The problem can be shown by considering a single-layer, single-neuron system with two inputs as shown in Figure 2-4. Calling one input x and the other y, all of their possible combinations comprise four points on the x–y plane shown in Figure 2-5. For example, the points $x = 0$ and $y = 0$ are labeled as point A_0 in the figure. Table 2-1 shows the desired relationships between inputs and outputs, where those input combinations that should produce a zero output are labeled A_0 and A_1; those producing a one are labeled B_0 and B_1.

In the network of Figure 2-4, function F is a simple threshold producing a zero for OUT when NET is below 0.5 and a one when

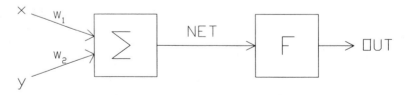

Figure 2-4.   Single-Neuron System

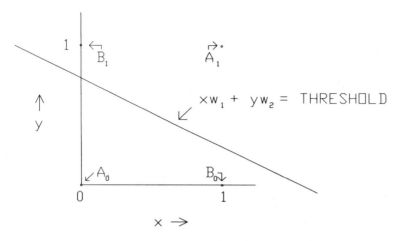

Figure 2-5. Exclusive-Or Problem as Points on the X–Y Plane

it is equal to or above it. The neuron then performs the following calculation:

$$NET = xw_1 + yw_2 \tag{2-1}$$

No combination of values for two weights w_1 and w_2 will produce the input/output relationship of Table 2-1. To understand this limitation, consider NET to be held constant at the threshold value of 0.5. Equation 2-2 describes the network in this case. This equation is linear in x and y; that is, all values for x and y that satisfy this equation will fall on some straight line on the x–y plane.

$$xw_1 + yw_2 = 0.5 \tag{2-2}$$

Table 2-1. Exclusive-Or Truth Table

Point	x Value	y Value	Desired Output
A_0	0	0	0
B_0	1	0	1
B_1	0	1	1
A_1	1	1	0

Any input values for x and y on this line will produce the threshold value of 0.5 for NET. Input values on one side of the line will produce NET greater than the threshold, hence OUT = 1; values on the other side will produce NET less than the threshold value making OUT = 0. Changing the values of w_1, w_2, and the threshold will change the slope and position of the line. For the network to produce the exclusive-or function of Table 2-1 it is necessary to place the line so that all of the As are on one side and all of the Bs are on the other. Try drawing such a line on Figure 2-5; it cannot be done. This means that no matter what values are assigned to the weights and the threshold, this network is unable to produce the input/output relationship required to represent the exclusive-or function.

Looking at the problem from a slightly different perspective, consider NET to be a surface floating above the x–y plane. Each point on this surface is directly above a corresponding point in the x–y plane by a distance equal to the value of NET at that point. It can be shown that the slope of this NET surface is constant over the entire x–y plane. All points that produce a value of NET equal to the threshold value will project up to a constant level on the NET plane (see Figure 2-6). Clearly, all points on one side of the threshold line will project up to values of NET higher than the threshold and points on the other side must result in lower values of NET. Thus, the threshold line subdivides the x–y plane into two

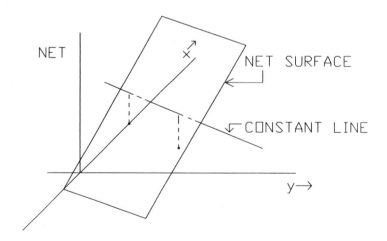

Figure 2-6.   Perceptron NET Plane

regions. All points on one side of the threshold line produce a one for OUT; all points on the other side produce a zero.

Linear Separability

We have seen that there is no way to draw a straight line subdividing the x–y plane so that the exclusive-or function is represented. Unfortunately, this is not an isolated example; there exists a large class of functions that cannot be represented by a single-layer network. These functions are said to be linearly inseparable, and they set definite bounds on the capabilities of single-layer networks.

Linear separability limits single-layer networks to classification problems in which the sets of points (corresponding to input values) can be separated geometrically. For our two-input case, the separator is a straight line. For three inputs, the separation is performed by a flat plane cutting through the resulting three-dimensional space. For four or more inputs, visualization breaks down and we must mentally generalize to a space of n dimensions divided by a "hyperplane," a geometrical object that subdivides a space of four or more dimensions.

Because linear separability limits the representational ability of a perceptron, it is important to know if a given function is linearly separable. Unfortunately, there is no simple way to make this determination if the number of variables is large.

A neuron with n binary inputs can have 2^n different input patterns, consisting of ones and zeros. Because each input pattern can produce two different binary outputs, one and zero, there are 2^{2^n} different functions of n variables.

As shown in Table 2-2, the probability of any randomly selected function being linearly separable becomes vanishingly small with even a modest number of variables. For this reason single-layer perceptrons are, in practice, limited to simple problems.

Overcoming the Linear Separability Limitation

By the late 1960s the linear separability problem was well understood. It was also known that this serious representational limita-

Table 2-2.   Linearly Separable Functions

n	2^{2^n}	Number of Linearly Separable Functions
1	4	4
2	16	14
3	256	104
4	65,536	1,882
5	4.3×10^9	94,572
6	1.8×10^{19}	5,028,134

Source: R. O. Windner, *Single-stage logic,* Paper presented at the AIEE Fall General Meeting (1960).

tion of single-layer networks could be overcome by adding more layers. For example, two-layer networks may be formed by cascading two single-layer networks. These can perform more general classifications, separating those points that are contained in convex open or closed regions. A convex region is one in which any two points in the region can be joined by a straight line that does not leave the region. A closed region is one in which all points are contained within a boundary (e.g., a circle). An open region has some points that are outside any defined boundary (e.g., the region between two parallel lines). For examples of convex open and closed regions, see Figure 2-7.

To understand the convexity limitation, consider a simple two-layer network with two inputs going to two neurons in the first layer, both feeding a single neuron in layer 2 (see Figure 2-8). Assume that the threshold of the output neuron is set at 0.75 and its weights are both set to 0.5. In this case, an output of one is required from both layer 1 neurons to exceed the threshold and to produce a one on the output. Thus, the output neuron performs a logical "and" function. In Figure 2-8 it is assumed that each neuron in layer 1 subdivides the x–y plane, one producing an output of one for inputs below the upper line and the other producing an output of one for inputs above the lower line. Figure 2-8 shows the result of the double subdivision, where the OUT of the layer 2 neuron is one only over a V-shaped region. Similarly, three neurons can be used in the input layer, further subdividing the plane, creat-

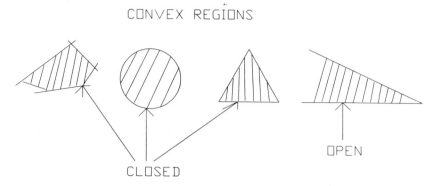

Figure 2-7.   Convex Regions, Closed and Open

ing a triangle-shaped region. By including enough neurons in the input layer, a convex polygon of any desired shape can be formed. Because they are formed by the "and" of regions defined by straight lines, all such polygons are convex, hence only convex regions can be enclosed. Points not comprising a convex region

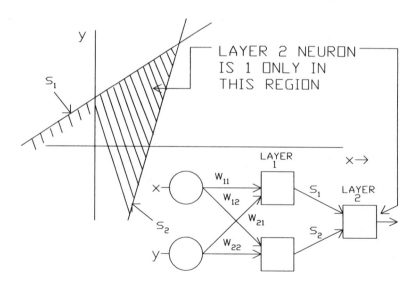

Figure 2-8. Convex Decision Region Produced by Two-Layer Per

cannot be separated from all other points in the plane by a two-layer network.

The layer 2 neuron is not limited to the "and" function; it can produce many other functions if the weights and threshold are suitably chosen. For example, it could be so arranged that either of the two neurons in layer 1 having a one for its OUT level causes the OUT level of the layer 2 neuron to be one, thereby forming a logical "or." There are 16 binary functions of two variables. If the weights and threshold are appropriately selected, a two-input neuron can simulate 14 of them (all but the exclusive-or and exclusive-nor).

Inputs need not be binary. A vector of continuous inputs can represent a point anywhere on the x–y plane. In this case, we are concerned with a network's ability to subdivide the plane into continuous regions rather than separating sets of discrete points. For all functions, however, linear separability shows that the output of a layer 2 neuron is one only over a portion of the x–y plane enclosed by a convex polygon. Thus, to separate regions P and Q, all points in P must be within a convex polygon that contains no points of Q (or vice versa).

A three-layer network is still more general; its classification capability is limited only by the number of artificial neurons and weights. There are no convexity constraints; the layer 3 neuron now receives as input a group of convex polygons, and the logical combination of that need not be convex. Figure 2-9 illustrates a case in which two triangles, A and B, are combined by the function "A and not B," thereby defining a nonconvex region. As neurons and weights are added, the number of sides of the polygons can increase without limit. This makes it possible to enclose a region of any shape to any desired degree of accuracy. In addition, not all of the layer 2 output regions need to intersect. It is possible, therefore, to enclose multiple regions, convex and nonconvex, producing an output of one whenever the input vector is in any of them.

Despite early recognition of the power of multilayer networks, for many years there was no theoretically sound training algorithm for adjusting their weights. In the chapters that follow we explore multilayer training algorithms in detail, but for now it is enough to understand the problem and to realize that research has produced solutions.

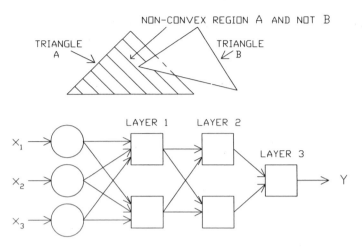

Figure 2-9. Concave Decision Region Formed by Intersection of Two Convex Regions

Storage Efficiency

There are serious questions about the storage efficiency of the perceptron (and other artificial neural networks) relative to conventional computer memory and retrieval methods. For example, it would be possible to store all of the input patterns in a computer's memory along with classification bits. The computer would then search for the desired pattern and respond with its classification. Various well-known strategies could be employed to accelerate the search. If an exact match were not found, nearest-neighbor criteria could be used to return the closest fit.

The number of bits required to store the same information in the perceptron weights can be substantially smaller than the conventional computer memory method, if the nature of the patterns allows a compact representation. However, Minsky (Minsky and Papert 1969) has shown pathological examples in which the number of bits required to represent the weights grows faster than exponentially with the size of the problem. In these cases, memory requirements quickly expand to impractical levels as the problem size increases. If, as he conjectures, this situation is not the exception, perceptrons could often be limited to small problems. How common are such infeasible pattern sets? This remains an open question that applies to all neural networks. Finding an answer is one of the critical areas for neural network research.

PERCEPTRON LEARNING

The artificial neural network's learning ability is its most intriguing property. Like the biological systems they model, these networks modify themselves as a result of experience to produce a more desirable behavior pattern.

Using the linear-separability criterion it is possible to decide whether or not a single-layer network can represent a desired function. Even if the answer is "Yes," it does us little good if we have no way to find the needed values for weights and thresholds. If the network is to be of practical value, we need a systematic method (an algorithm) for computing the values. Rosenblatt (1962) provided this in the perceptron training algorithm, along with his proof that a perceptron can be trained to any function it can represent.

Learning can be either supervised or unsupervised. Supervised learning requires an external "teacher" that evaluates the behavior of the system and directs the subsequent modifications. Unsupervised learning, which is covered in the chapters that follow, requires no teacher; the network self-organizes to produce the desired changes. Perceptron learning is of the supervised type.

The perceptron training algorithm can be implemented on a digital computer or other electronic hardware and the network becomes, in a sense, self-adjusting. For this reason the act of adjusting the weights is commonly called "training," and the network is said to "learn." Rosenblatt's proof was a major milestone and provided a great impetus to research in the field. Today, in one form or another, elements of the perceptron training algorithm are found in many modern network paradigms.

PERCEPTRON TRAINING ALGORITHM

A perceptron is trained by presenting a set of patterns to its input, one at a time, and adjusting the weights until the desired output occurs for each of them. Suppose that the input patterns are on flash cards. Each flash card can be marked into squares, and each square can provide an input to the perceptron. If a square has a line through it, its output is one; if not, its output is zero. The set of squares on a card represents the set of ones and zeros presented as inputs to the perceptron. The object is to train the perceptron so that applying a set of inputs representing an odd number always turns the light on, while it remains off for even numbers.

Figure 2-10 shows such a perceptron configuration. Suppose that the vector $\mathbf{X}$ represents the flash card pattern to be recognized. Each component (square) of $\mathbf{X}$, $(x_1, x_2, \ldots, x_n)$, is multiplied by its corresponding component of weight vector $\mathbf{W}$, $(w_1, w_2, \ldots, w_n)$. These products are summed. If the sum exceeds a threshold θ, the output of the neuron Y is one (and the light is on), otherwise it is zero. As we have seen in Chapter 1, this operation may be represented compactly in vector form as $Y = \mathbf{XW}$, followed by the thresholding operation.

To train the network, a pattern $\mathbf{X}$ is applied to the input and the output Y is calculated. If Y is correct, nothing is changed. Howev-

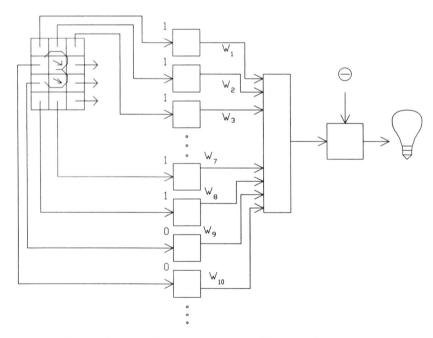

Figure 2-10. Perceptron Image-Recognition System

er, if the output is incorrect, the weights connecting to inputs enhancing this erroneous result are modified in value to reduce the error.

To see how this is accomplished, assume that a flash card bearing the number three is input to the system and the output Y is one (indicating odd). Since this is the correct response, no weights are changed. If, however, a flash card with the number four is input to the perceptron and the output Y is one (odd), the weights that connect to inputs that are one must be decreased, as these are tending to produce an incorrect result. Similarly, if a card with the number three produces an output of zero, those weights connecting to inputs that are one must be increased, thereby tending to correct this erroneous condition.

This training method can be summarized:

1. Apply an input pattern and calculate the output Y.
2.
   a. If the output is correct, go to step 1;
   b. If the output is incorrect, and is zero, add each input to its corresponding weight; or
   c. If the output is incorrect and is one, subtract each input from its corresponding weight.
3. Go to step 1.

In a finite number of steps the network will learn to separate the cards into even and odd categories, provided that the sets of figures are linearly separable. That is, for all odd cards the output will be higher than the threshold, and for all even cards it will be below it. Note that this training is global; that is, the network learns over the entire set of cards. This raises questions about how the set should be presented to minimize the training time. Should the set be applied sequentially, over and over, or should cards be selected at random? There is little theory to guide this determination.

The Delta Rule

An important generalization of the perceptron training algorithm, called the delta rule, extends this technique to continuous inputs and outputs. To see how it was developed, note that step 2 of the perceptron training algorithm may be restated and generalized by introducing a term δ, which is the difference between the desired or target output T and the actual output A. In symbols,

$$\delta = (T - A) \tag{2-3}$$

The case in which $\delta = 0$ corresponds to step 2a, in which the output is correct and nothing is done. Step 2b corresponds to $\delta > 0$, while step 2c corresponds to $\delta < 0$.

In any of these cases, the perceptron training algorithm is satisfied if δ is multiplied by the value of each input x_i and this product is added to the corresponding weight. To generalize this, a "learning rate" coefficient η multiplies the δx_i product to allow control of the average size of weight changes.

Symbolically,

$$\Delta_i = \eta \, \delta \, x_i \tag{2-4}$$

$$w_i(n + 1) = w_i(n) + \Delta_i \tag{2-5}$$

where

Δ_i = the correction associated with the ith input x_i
$w_i(n + 1)$ = the value of weight i after adjustment
$w_i(n)$ = the value of weight i before adjustment

The delta rule modifies weights appropriately for target and actual outputs of either polarity and for both continuous and binary inputs and outputs. These characteristics have opened up a wealth of new applications.

Problems with the Perceptron Training Algorithm

It may be difficult to determine if the caveat regarding linear separability is satisfied for the particular training set at hand. Furthermore, in many real-world situations the inputs are often time-varying and may be separable at one time and not at another. Also, there is no statement in the proof of the perceptron learning algorithm that indicates how many steps will be required to train the network. It is small consolation to know that training will only take a finite number of steps if the time it takes is measured in geological units. Furthermore, there is no proof that the perceptron training algorithm is faster than simply trying all possible adjustments of the weights; in some cases this brute-force approach may be superior.

These questions have never been satisfactorily answered, and they are certainly related to the nature of the set being learned. They are asked in various forms in the chapters that follow, as they apply to other network paradigms. Generally, the answers are no more satisfactory for more modern networks than they are for the perceptrons. These problems represent important areas of current research.

References

McCulloch, W. W., and Pitts, W. 1943. A logical calculus of the ideas imminent in nervous activity. *Bulletin of Mathematical Biophysics* 5:115–33.

Minsky, M. L., and Papert S. 1969. *Perceptrons*. Cambridge, MA: MIT Press.

Pitts, W., and McCulloch, W. W. 1947. How we know universals. *Bulletin of Mathematical Biophysics* 9:127–47.

Rosenblatt, F. 1962. *Principles of neurodynamics*. New York: Spartan Books.

Widrow, B. 1961. *The speed of adaptation in adaptive control systems*, paper #1933-61. American Rocket Society Guidance Control and Navigation Conference.

———. 1963. A statistical theory of adaptation. *Adaptive control systems*. New York: Pergamon Press.

Widrow, B., and Angell, J. B. 1962. Reliable, trainable networks for computing and control. *Aerospace Engineering* 21:78–123.

Widrow, B., and Hoff, M. E. 1960. Adaptive switching circuits. *1960 IRE WESCON Convention Record*, part 4, pp. 96–104. New York: Institute of Radio Engineers.

3

Backpropagation

INTRODUCTION TO BACKPROPAGATION

For many years there was no theoretically sound algorithm for training multilayer artificial neural networks. Since single-layer networks proved severely limited in what they could represent (hence, in what they could learn), the entire field went into virtual eclipse.

The invention of the backpropagation algorithm has played a large part in the resurgence of interest in artificial neural networks. Backpropagation is a systematic method for training multilayer artificial neural networks. It has a mathematical foundation that is strong if not highly practical. Despite its limitations, backpropagation has dramatically expanded the range of problems to which artificial neural networks can be applied, and it has generated many successful demonstrations of its power.

Backpropagation has an interesting history. Rumelhart, Hinton, and Williams (1986) presented a clear and concise description of the backpropagation algorithm. No sooner was this work published than Parker (1982) was shown to have anticipated Rumelhart's work. Shortly after this, Werbos (1974) was found to have described the method still earlier. Rumelhart and Parker could have saved a great deal of effort if they had been aware of Werbos's work. Although similar duplication of effort is found in virtually every scientific discipline, in artificial neural networks the problem is particularly severe due to the interdisciplinary nature of the subject. Neural-network research is published in books and journals from such diverse fields that even the most diligent researcher is hard pressed to remain aware of all significant work.

THE BACKPROPAGATION TRAINING ALGORITHM

Network Configurations

The Neuron

Figure 3-1 shows the neuron used as the fundamental building block for backpropagation networks. A set of inputs is applied, either from the outside or from a previous layer. Each of these is multiplied by a weight, and the products are summed. This summation of products is termed *NET* and must be calculated for each neuron in the network. After NET is calculated, an activation function *F* is applied to modify it, thereby producing the signal *OUT*.

Figure 3-2 shows the activation function usually used for backpropagation.

$$OUT = 1/(1 + e^{-NET}) \tag{3-1}$$

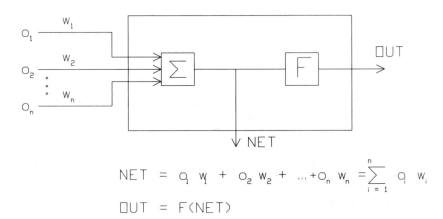

$$NET = O_1 W_1 + O_2 W_2 + \dots + O_n W_n = \sum_{i=1}^{n} O_i W_i$$

$$OUT = F(NET)$$

Figure 3-1. Artificial Neuron with Activation Function

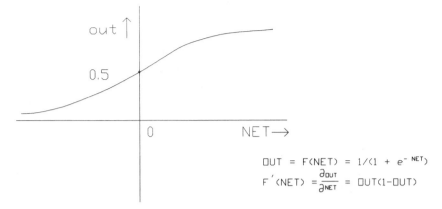

$$\text{OUT} = F(\text{NET}) = 1/(1 + e^{-\text{NET}})$$
$$F'(\text{NET}) = \frac{\partial_{\text{OUT}}}{\partial_{\text{NET}}} = \text{OUT}(1-\text{OUT})$$

Figure 3-2. Sigmoidal Activation Function

As shown by Equation 3-2, this function, called a *sigmoid*, is desirable in that it has a simple derivative, a fact we use in implementing the backpropagation algorithm.

$$\frac{\partial \text{ OUT}}{\partial \text{ NET}} = \text{OUT}(1 - \text{OUT}) \tag{3-2}$$

Sometimes called a *logistic*, or simply a *squashing function*, the sigmoid compresses the range of NET so that OUT lies between zero and one. As discussed previously, multilayer networks have greater representational power than single-layer networks only if a nonlinearity is introduced. The squashing function produces the needed nonlinearity.

There are many functions that might be used; the backpropagation algorithm requires only that the function be everywhere differentiable. The sigmoid satisfies this requirement. It has the additional advantage of providing a form of automatic gain control. For small signals (NET near zero) the slope of the input/output curve is steep, producing high gain. As the magnitude of the signal becomes greater, the gain decreases. In this way large signals can be accommodated by the network without saturation, while small signals are allowed to pass through without excessive attenuation.

The Multilayer Network

Figure 3-3 shows a multilayer network suitable for training with backpropagation. (The figure has been simplified for clarity.) The first set of neurons (connecting to the inputs) serve only as distribution points; they perform no input summation. The input signal is simply passed through to the weights on their outputs. Each neuron in subsequent layers produces NET and OUT signals as described above.

The literature is inconsistent in defining the number of layers in these networks. Some authors refer to the number of layers of neurons (including the nonsumming input layer), others to the layers of weights. Because the latter definition is more functionally descriptive, it is used throughout this book. By this definition, the network of Figure 3-3 is considered to consist of two layers. Also, a neuron is associated with the set of weights that connects to its input. Thus, the weights in layer 1 terminate on the neurons of layer 1. The input or distribution layer is designated layer 0.

Backpropagation can be applied to networks with any number of layers; however, only two layers of weights are needed to demonstrate the algorithm. At this point in the discussion, only feedforward networks are considered. It is quite possible to apply

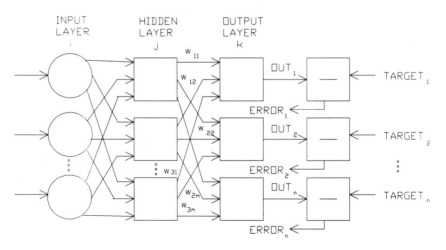

Figure 3-3.   Two-Layer Backpropagation Network

backpropagation to networks with feedback connections; these are discussed later in this chapter.

An Overview of Training

The objective of training the network is to adjust the weights so that application of a set of inputs produces the desired set of outputs. For reasons of brevity, these input–output sets can be referred to as *vectors*. Training assumes that each input vector is paired with a target vector representing the desired output; together these are called a *training pair*. Usually, a network is trained over a number of training pairs. For example, the input part of a training pair might consist of a pattern of ones and zeros representing a binary image of a letter of the alphabet. Figure 3-4 shows a set of inputs for the letter A drawn on a grid. If a line passes through a square, the corresponding neuron's input is one; otherwise, that neuron's input is zero. The output might be a number that represents the letter A, or perhaps another set of ones and zeros that could be used to produce an output pattern. If one wished to train the network to recognize all the letters of the alphabet, 26 training pairs would be required. This group of training pairs is called a *training set*.

Before starting the training process, all of the weights must be initialized to small random numbers. This ensures that the network is not saturated by large values of the weights, and prevents certain other training pathologies. For example, if the weights all start at equal values and the desired performance requires unequal values, the network will not learn.

Training the backpropagation network requires the steps that follow:

1. Select the next training pair from the training set; apply the input vector to the network input.
2. Calculate the output of the network.
3. Calculate the error between the network output and the desired output (the target vector from the training pair).
4. Adjust the weights of the network in a way that minimizes the error.

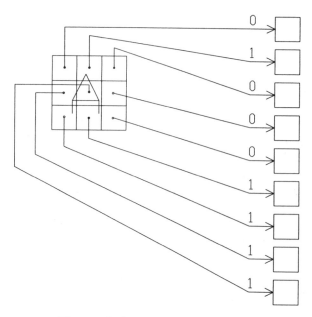

Figure 3-4.   Image Recognition

5. Repeat steps 1 through 4 for each vector in the training set until the error for the entire set is acceptably low.

The operations required in steps 1 and 2 above are similar to the way in which the trained network will ultimately be used; that is, an input vector is applied and the resulting output is calculated. Calculations are performed on a layer-by-layer basis. Referring to Figure 3-3, first the outputs of the neurons in layer j are calculated; these are then used as inputs to layer k; the layer k neuron outputs are calculated and these constitute the network output vector.

In step 3, each of the network outputs, labeled OUT in Figure 3-3, is subtracted from its corresponding component of the target vector to produce an error. This error is used in step 4 to adjust the weights of the network, where the polarity and magnitude of the weight changes are determined by the training algorithm (see below).

After enough repetitions of these four steps, the error between actual outputs and target outputs should be reduced to an acceptable value, and the network is said to be trained. At this point, the network is used for recognition and weights are not changed.

It may be seen that steps 1 and 2 constitute a "forward pass" in that the signal propagates from the network input to its output. Steps 3 and 4 are a "reverse pass"; here, the calculated error signal propagates backward through the network where it is used to adjust weights. These two passes are now expanded and expressed in a somewhat more mathematical form.

Forward Pass

Steps 1 and 2 can be expressed in vector form as follows: an input vector **X** is applied and an output vector **Y** is produced. The input-target vector pair **X** and **T** comes from the training set. The calculation is performed on **X** to produce the output vector **Y**.

As we have seen, calculation in multilayer networks is done layer by layer, starting at the layer nearest to the inputs. The NET value of each neuron in the first layer is calculated as the weighted sum of its neuron's inputs. The activation function F then "squashes" NET to produce the OUT value for each neuron in that layer. Once the set of outputs for a layer is found, it serves as input to the next layer. The process is repeated, layer by layer, until the final set of network outputs is produced.

This process can be stated succinctly in vector notation. The weights between neurons can be considered to be a matrix **W**. For example, the weight from neuron 8 in layer 2 to neuron 5 in layer 3 is designated $w_{8,5}$. Rather than using the summation of products, the NET vector for a layer **N** may be expressed as the product of **X** and **W**. In vector notation **N** = **XW**. Applying the function F to the NET vector **N**, component by component, produces the output vector **O**. Thus, for a given layer, the following expression describes the calculation process:

$$\mathbf{O} = F(\mathbf{XW}) \qquad (3\text{-}3)$$

The output vector for one layer is the input vector for the next, so calculating the outputs of the final layer requires the application of Equation 3-3 to each layer, from the network's input to its output.

Reverse Pass

Adjusting the Weights of the Output Layer.   Because a target value is available for each neuron in the output layer, adjusting the associated weights is easily accomplished using a modification of the delta rule presented in Chapter 2. Interior layers are referred to as "hidden layers," as their outputs have no target values for comparison; hence, training is more complicated.

Figure 3-5 shows the training process for a single weight from neuron p in the hidden layer j to neuron q in the output layer k. The output of a neuron in layer k is subtracted from its target value to produce an ERROR signal. This is multiplied by the derivative of the squashing function [OUT(1−OUT)] calculated for that layer's neuron k, thereby producing the δ value.

$$\delta = \text{OUT}(1-\text{OUT})\,(\text{Target}-\text{OUT}) \tag{3-4}$$

Then δ is multiplied by OUT from a neuron j, the source neuron for the weight in question. This product is in turn multiplied by a training rate coefficient η (typically 0.01 to 1.0) and the result is added to the weight. An identical process is performed for each weight proceeding from a neuron in the hidden layer to a neuron in the output layer.

The following equations illustrate this calculation:

$$\Delta\,w_{pq,k} = \eta\,\delta_{q,k}\,\text{OUT}_{p,j} \tag{3-5}$$

$$w_{pq,k}(n+1) = w_{pq,k}(n) + \Delta\,w_{pq,k} \tag{3-6}$$

where

$w_{pq,k}(n)$ = the value of a weight from neuron p in the hidden layer to neuron q in the output layer at step n (before adjustment); note that the subscript k indicates that the weight is associated with its destination layer, a convention followed in this book

$w_{pq,k}(n+1)$ = value of the weight at step $n+1$ (after adjustment)

$\delta_{q,k}$ = the value of δ for neuron q in the output layer k

$\text{OUT}_{p,j}$ = the value of OUT for neuron p in the hidden layer j.

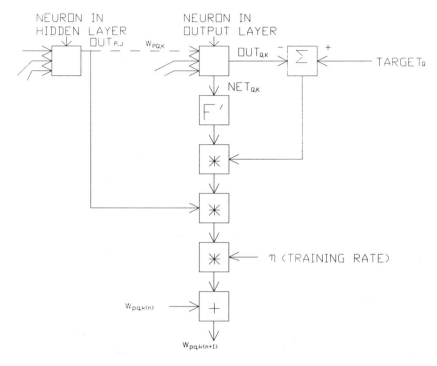

Figure 3-5.   Training a Weight in the Output Layer

Note that subscripts p and q refer to a specific neuron, whereas subscripts j and k refer to a layer.

Adjusting the Weights of the Hidden Layers.   Hidden layers have no target vector, so the training process described above cannot be used. This lack of a training target stymied efforts to train multilayer networks until backpropagation provided a workable algorithm. Backpropagation trains the hidden layers by propagating the output error back through the network layer by layer, adjusting weights at each layer.

Equations 3-5 and 3-6 are used for all layers, both output and hidden; however, for hidden layers δ must be generated without benefit of a target vector. Figure 3-6 shows how this is accomplished. First, δ is calculated for each neuron in the output layer, as

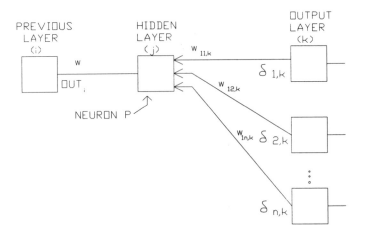

Figure 3-6. Training a Weight in a Hidden Layer

in Equation 3-4. It is used to adjust the weights feeding into the output layer, then it is propagated back through the same weights to generate a value for δ for each neuron in the first hidden layer. These values of δ are used, in turn, to adjust the weights of this hidden layer and, in a similar way, are propagated back to all preceding layers.

Consider a single neuron in the hidden layer just before the output layer. In the forward pass, this neuron propagates its output value to neurons in the output layer through the interconnecting weights. During training these weights operate in reverse, passing the value of δ from the output layer back to the hidden layer. Each of these weights is multiplied by the δ value of the neuron to which it connects in the output layer. The value of δ needed for the hidden-layer neuron is produced by summing all such products and multiplying by the derivative of the squashing function:

$$\delta_{p,j} = \text{OUT}_{p,j}(1 - \text{OUT}_{p,j}) \left(\sum_q \delta_{q,k}\, w_{pq,k} \right) \qquad (3\text{-}7)$$

(See Figure 3-6.) With δ in hand, the weights feeding the first hidden layer can be adjusted using Equations 3-5 and 3-6, modifying indices to indicate the correct layers.

For each neuron in a given hidden layer, δs must be calculated, and all weights associated with that layer must be adjusted. This is repeated, moving back toward the input layer by layer, until all weights are adjusted.

With vector notation, the operation of propagating the error back can be expressed much more compactly. Call the set of δs at the output layer $\mathbf{D}_k$ and the set of weights for the output layer the array $\mathbf{W}_k$. To arrive at $\mathbf{D}_j$, the δ vector for the hidden layer, the two steps that follow will suffice:

1. Multiply the δ vector of the output layer $\mathbf{D}_k$ by the transpose of the weight matrix connecting the hidden layer to the output layer $\mathbf{W}_k^t$.
2. Multiply each component of the resulting product by the derivative of the squashing function for the corresponding neuron in the hidden layer.

Symbolically,

$$\mathbf{D}_j = \mathbf{D}_k \mathbf{W}_k^t \; \$ \; [\mathbf{O}_j \; \$ \; (\mathbf{I} - \mathbf{O}_j)] \qquad (3\text{-}8)$$

where, for the purposes of this book, the operator $ is defined to indicate component-by-component multiplication of the two vectors. $\mathbf{O}_j$ is the output vector of layer j, and $\mathbf{I}$ is a vector, all components of which are 1.

Adding a Neuron Bias

In many cases it is desirable to provide each neuron with a trainable bias. This offsets the origin of the logistic function, producing an effect that is similar to adjusting the threshold of the perceptron neuron, thereby permitting more rapid convergence of the training process. This feature is easily incorporated into the training algorithm; a weight connected to + 1 is added to each neuron. This weight is trainable in the same way as all of the other weights, except that the source is always + 1 instead of being the output of a neuron in a previous layer.

Momentum

Rumelhart, Hinton, and Williams (1986) describe a method for improving the training time of the backpropagation algorithm, while enhancing the stability of the process. Called *momentum*, the method involves adding a term to the weight adjustment that is proportional to the amount of the previous weight change. Once an adjustment is made it is "remembered" and serves to modify all subsequent weight adjustments. The adjustment equations are modified to the following:

$$\Delta w_{pq,k}(n + 1) = \eta \, (\delta_{q,k} \, \text{OUT}_{p,j}) + \alpha[\Delta \, w_{pq,k}(n)] \qquad (3\text{-}9)$$

$$w_{pq,k}(n + 1) = w_{pq,k}(n) + \Delta \, w_{pq,k}(n + 1) \qquad (3\text{-}10)$$

where α, the momentum coefficient, is commonly set to around 0.9.

Using the momentum method, the network tends to follow the bottom of narrow gullies in the error surface (if they exist) rather than crossing rapidly from side to side. This method seems to work well on some problems, but it has little or negative effect on others.

Sejnowski and Rosenberg (1987) describe a similar method based on exponential smoothing that may prove superior in some applications.

$$\Delta w_{pq,k}(n + 1) = \alpha \, \Delta \, w_{pq,k}(n) + (1 - \alpha) \, \delta_{q,k} \, \text{OUT}_{p,j} \qquad (3\text{-}11)$$

Then the weight change is computed:

$$w_{pq,k}(n + 1) = w_{pq,k}(n) + \eta \, \Delta \, w_{pq,k}(n + 1) \qquad (3\text{-}12)$$

where α is a smoothing coefficient in the range of 0.0 to 1.0. If α is 0.0, then smoothing is minimum; the entire weight adjustment comes from the newly calculated change. If α is 1.0, the new adjustment is ignored and the previous one is repeated. Between 0 and 1 is a region where the weight adjustment is smoothed by an amount proportional to α. Again η is the training-rate coefficient, serving to adjust the size of the average weight change.

ADVANCED ALGORITHMS

Many researchers have devised improvements and extensions to the basic backpropagation algorithm described above. The literature is far too extensive to cover here. Furthermore, it is much too early for a full evaluation; some of these techniques may prove to be fundamental, others may simply fade away. For reference, a few of the more promising developments are discussed in this section.

Parker (1987) describes a method for improving the speed of convergence of the backpropagation algorithm. Called *second-order backpropagation*, it uses second derivatives to produce a more accurate estimate of the correct weight change. Parker has shown that the algorithm is optimal in the sense that using higher-than-second-order derivatives will not improve the estimate. Computational requirements are increased compared to first-order backpropagation, and more test results are needed to prove that the additional cost is justified.

Stornetta and Huberman (1987) describe a deceptively simple method for improving the training characteristics of backpropagation networks. They point out that the conventional 0-to-1 dynamic range of inputs and hidden neuron outputs is not optimum. Because the magnitude of a weight adjustment $\Delta w_{pq,k}$ is proportional to the output level of the neuron from which it originates $OUT_{p,j}$, a level of 0 results in no weight modification. With binary input vectors, half the inputs, on the average, will be 0 and the weights they connect to will not train! The solution lies in changing the input range to $\pm 1/2$ and adding a bias to the squashing function to modify the neuron output range to $\pm 1/2$. The new squashing function is as follows:

$$OUT = -1/2 + 1/(e^{-NET} + 1) \qquad (3\text{-}13)$$

Convergence times were reduced by an average of 30 to 50% with these easily implemented changes. This is an example of the practical modifications that can bring substantial improvements in the algorithm's performance.

Pineda (1988) and Almeida (1987) have described methods for applying backpropagation to recurrent networks, that is, networks whose outputs feedback to inputs. They show that learning can occur very rapidly in such systems and that stability criteria are easily satisfied.

APPLICATIONS

Backpropagation has been applied to a wide variety of research applications; a few of these are described to demonstrate the power of this method.

NEC in Japan has announced recently that it has applied backpropagation to a new optical-character-recognition system, thereby improving accuracy to over 99%. This improvement was achieved through a combination of conventional algorithms with a backpropagation network providing additional verification.

Sejnowski and Rosenberg (1987) produced a spectacular success with NetTalk, a system that converted printed English text into highly intelligible speech. His tape recording of the training process bore a strong resemblance to the sounds of a child at various stages of learning to speak.

Burr (1987) has used backpropagation in machine recognition of handwritten English words. The characters are normalized for size, are placed on a grid, and projections are made of the lines through the squares of the grid. These projections then form the inputs to a backpropagation network. He reports accuracies of 99.7% when used with a dictionary filter.

Cottrell, Munro, and Zipser (1987) report a successful image-compression application in which images were represented with one bit per pixel, an eightfold improvement over the input data.

CAVEATS

Despite the many successful applications of backpropagation, it is not a panacea. Most troublesome is the long, uncertain training process. For complex problems it may require days or weeks to train the network, and it may not train at all. Long training time can be the result of a nonoptimum step size. Outright training failures generally arise from two sources: network paralysis and local minima.

Network Paralysis

As the network trains, the weights can become adjusted to very large values. This can force all or most of the neurons to operate at large values of OUT, in a region where the derivative of the squashing function is very small. Since the error sent back for training is proportional to this derivative, the training process can come to a virtual standstill. There is little theoretical understanding of this problem. It is commonly avoided by reducing the step size η, but this extends training time. Various heuristics have been employed to prevent paralysis, or to recover from its effects, but these can only be described as experimental.

Local Minima

Backpropagation employs a type of gradient descent; that is, it follows the slope of the error surface downward, constantly adjusting the weights toward a minimum. The error surface of a complex network is highly convoluted, full of hills, valleys, folds, and gullies in high-dimensional space. The network can get trapped in a local minimum (a shallow valley) when there is a much deeper minimum nearby. From the limited viewpoint of the network, all directions are up, and it has no way to escape. Statistical training methods can help avoid this trap, but they tend to be slow. Wasserman (1988a) has proposed a method that combines the statistical methods of the Cauchy machine with the gradient descent of backpropagation to produce a system that finds global minima while retaining the higher training rate of backpropagation. This is discussed in Chapter 5.

Step Size

A careful reading of the convergence proof of Rumelhart, Hinton, and Williams (1986) shows that infinitesimally small weight adjustments are assumed. This is clearly impractical, as it implies infinite training time. It is necessary to select a finite step size, and there is very little to guide that decision other than experience. If the step size is too small, convergence can be very slow; if too large, paralysis or continuous instability can result. Wasserman (1988b) describes an adaptive step size algorithm intended to adjust step size automatically as the training process proceeds.

Temporal Instability

If a network is learning to recognize the alphabet, it does no good to learn B if, in so doing, it forgets A. A process is needed for teaching the network to learn an entire training set without disrupting what it has already learned. Rumelhart's convergence proof accomplishes this but requires that the network be shown all vectors in the training set before adjusting any weights. The needed weight changes must be accumulated over the entire set, thereby requiring additional storage. After a number of such training cycles, the weights will converge to a minimal error. This method may not be useful if the network faces a continuously changing environment where it may never see the same input vector twice. In this case, the training process may never converge; it may wander aimlessly or oscillate wildly. In this sense backpropagation fails to mimic biological systems. As we point out in Chapter 8, this discrepancy (among others) led to Grossberg's ART system.

References

Almeida, L. B. 1987. Neural computers. *Proceedings of the NATO ARW on Neural Computers, Dusseldorf.* Heidelberg: Springer-Verlag.

Burr, D. J. 1987. Experiments with a connectionist text reader. In *Proceedings of the IEEE First International Conference on Neural Networks,* eds. M. Caudill and C. Butler, vol. 4, pp. 717–24. San Diego, CA: SOS Printing.

Cottrell, G. W., Munro, P., and Zipser, D. 1987. *Image compression by backpropagation: An example of extensional programming.* ICS Report 8702, University of California, San Diego.

Parker, D. B. 1982. *Learning logic.* Invention Report S81-64, File 1, Office of Technology Licensing, Stanford University, Stanford, CA.

_____. 1987. *Second order back propagation: Implementing an optimal O(n) approximation to Newton's method as an artificial neural network.* Manuscript submitted for publication.

Pineda, F. J. 1988. Generalization of backpropagation to recurrent and higher order networks. In *Neural information processing systems*, ed. Dana Z. Anderson, pp. 602–11. New York: American Institute of Physics.

Rumelhart, D. E., Hinton, G. E., and Williams, R.J. 1986. Learning internal representations by error propagation. In *Parallel distributed processing*, vol. 1, pp. 318–62. Cambridge, MA: MIT Press.

Sejnowski, T. J., and Rosenberg, C. R. 1987. Parallel networks that learn to pronounce English text. *Complex Systems* 1:145–68.

Stornetta, W. S., and Huberman, B. A. 1987. An improved three-layer, backpropagation algorithm. In *Proceedings of the IEEE First International Conference on Neural Networks,* eds. M. Caudill and C. Butler. San Diego, CA: SOS Printing.

Wasserman, P. D. 1988a. Combined backpropagation/Cauchy machine. *Proceedings of the International Neural Network Society.* New York: Pergamon Press.

———. 1988b. Experiments in translating Chinese characters using backpropagation. *Proceedings of the Thirty-Third IEEE Computer Society International Conference.* Washington, D.C.: Computer Society Press of the IEEE.

Werbos, P. J. 1974. *Beyond regression: New tools for prediction and analysis in the behavioral sciences.* Masters thesis, Harvard University.

4

Counterpropagation Networks

INTRODUCTION TO COUNTERPROPAGATION NETWORKS

The counterpropagation network developed by Robert Hecht-Nielsen (1987a, 1987b, 1988) goes beyond the representational limits of single-layer networks. As compared to backpropagation, it can reduce training time by one hundredfold. Counterpropagation is not as general as backpropagation, but it provides a solution for those applications that cannot tolerate long training sessions. We point out that in addition to overcoming the limitations of other networks, counterpropagation has some interesting and useful features of its own.

Counterpropagation is a combination of two well-known algorithms: the self-organizing map of Kohonen (1988) and the Grossberg (1969, 1971, 1982) outstar (see Appendix C). Together they possess properties not available in either one alone.

Methods such as counterpropagation that combine network paradigms in building-block fashion may produce networks closer to the brain's architecture than any homogeneous structure. It does indeed seem that the brain cascades various specialized modules to produce the desired computation.

The counterpropagation network functions as a look-up table capable of generalization. The training process associates input vectors with corresponding output vectors. These vectors may be binary, consisting of ones and zeros, or continuous. Once the network is trained, application of an input vector produces the desired output vector. The generalization capability of the network allows it to produce a correct output even when it is given an input vector that is partially incomplete or partially incorrect. This makes the network useful for pattern-recognition, pattern-completion, and signal-enhancement applications.

NETWORK STRUCTURE

Figure 4-1 shows the simplified feedforward version of the counterpropagation network; it illustrates the functional characteristics of this paradigm. The full bidirectional network uses the same principles and is discussed later in this chapter.

The neurons in layer 0 (shown as circles) serve only as fan-out points and perform no computation. Each layer-0 neuron connects to every neuron in layer 1 (called the Kohonen layer) through a separate weight w_{mn}; these will be collectively referred to as the weight matrix **W**. Similarly, each neuron in the Kohonen layer (layer 1) connects to every neuron in the Grossberg layer (layer 2) by a weight v_{np}; these comprise the weight matrix **V**. This looks much like other networks we have seen in earlier chapters; howev-

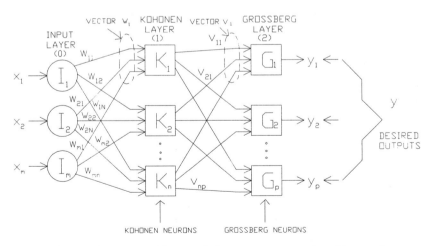

Figure 4-1.   Feedforward Counterpropagation Network

er, the difference lies in the processing done by the Kohonen and Grossberg neurons.

As in many other networks, counterpropagation functions in two modes: the normal mode, in which it accepts an input vector **X** and produces an output vector **Y**, and the training mode, in which an input vector is applied and the weights are adjusted to yield the desired output vector.

NORMAL OPERATION

Kohonen Layer

In its simplest form, the Kohonen layer functions in a "winner-take-all fashion"; that is, for a given input vector, one and only one Kohonen neuron outputs a logical one; all others output a zero. One can think of the Kohonen neurons as a series of light bulbs, only one of which comes on for a given input vector.

Associated with each Kohonen neuron is a set of weights connecting it to each input. For example, in Figure 4-1, Kohonen neuron K_1 has weights w_{11}, w_{21}, ..., w_{m1}, comprising a weight vector $\mathbf{W}_1$. These connect by way of the input layer to input signals $x_1, x_2, \ldots, x_m$, comprising the input vector **X**. As with neurons in most networks, the NET output of each Kohonen neuron is simply the summation of the weighted inputs. This may be expressed as follows:

$$\text{NET}_j = w_{1j}\, x_1 + w_{2j}\, x_2 + \ \ldots \ + w_{mj}\, x_m \qquad (4\text{-}1)$$

where NET_j is the NET output of Kohonen neuron j

$$\text{NET}_j = \sum_i x_i\, w_{ij} \qquad (4\text{-}2)$$

or in vector notation

$$\mathbf{N} = \mathbf{XW} \qquad (4\text{-}3)$$

where **N** is the vector of Kohonen layer NET outputs.

The Kohonen neuron with the largest NET value is the "winner." Its output is set to one; all others are set to zero.

Grossberg Layer

The Grossberg layer functions in a familiar manner. Its NET output is the weighted sum of the Kohonen layer outputs $k_1, k_2, \ldots, k_n$, forming the vector $\mathbf{K}$. The connecting weight vector designated $\mathbf{V}$ consists of the weights $v_{11}, v_{21}, \ldots, v_{np}$. The NET output of each Grossberg neuron is then

$$\text{NET}_j = \sum_i k_i w_{ij} \qquad (4\text{-}4)$$

where NET_j is the output of Grossberg neuron j, or in vector form

$$\mathbf{Y} = \mathbf{KV} \qquad (4\text{-}5)$$

where
  $\mathbf{Y}$ = the Grossberg-layer output vector
  $\mathbf{K}$ = the Kohonen-layer output vector
  $\mathbf{V}$ = the Grossberg layer weight matrix

If the Kohonen layer is operated such that only one neuron's NET is at one and all others are at zero, only one element of the $\mathbf{K}$ vector is nonzero, and the calculation is simple. In fact, the only action of each neuron in the Grossberg layer is to output the value of the weight that connects it to the single nonzero Kohonen neuron.

TRAINING THE KOHONEN LAYER

The Kohonen layer classifies the input vectors into groups that are similar. This is accomplished by adjusting the Kohonen layer weights so that similar input vectors activate the same Kohonen neuron. It is then the responsibility of the Grossberg layer to produce the desired outputs.

Kohonen training is a self-organizing algorithm that operates in the unsupervised mode. For this reason, it is difficult (and unnecessary) to predict which specific Kohonen neuron will be activated for a given input vector. It is only necessary to ensure that training separates dissimilar input vectors.

Preprocessing the Input Vectors

It is highly desirable (but not mandatory) to normalize all input vectors before applying them to the network. This is done by dividing each component of an input vector by that vector's length. This length is found by taking the square root of the sum of the squares of all of the vector's components. In symbols

$$x_i' = x_i/(x_1^2 + x_2^2 + \ldots + x_n^2)^{1/2} \tag{4-6}$$

This converts an input vector into a unit vector pointing in the same direction; that is, a vector of unit length in n-dimensional space.

Equation 4-6 generalizes the familiar two-dimensional case in which the length of a vector equals the hypotenuse of the right triangle formed by its x and y components, an application of the familiar Pythagorean theorem. In Figure 4-2a, such a two-dimen-

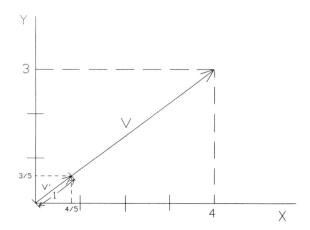

Figure 4-2a.   Unit Input Vector

sional vector **V** is drawn on x–y coordinates, where **V** has x and y components of four and three, respectively. The square root of the sum of the squares of these components is five. Dividing each component of **V** by five yields a vector **V'** with components 4/5 and 3/5 where **V'** points in the same direction as **V**, but is of unit length. This may be verified by calculating the square root of the sum of the squares of the components **V'**, which equals one.

Figure 4-2b shows some two-dimensional unit vectors. These terminate at points on a unit circle (a circle with a radius of one), which is the situation if there are only two inputs to the network. With three inputs, vectors would be represented as arrows terminating on the surface of a unit sphere. This idea can be extended to networks having an arbitrary number of inputs, where each input vector is an arrow terminating on the surface of a higher dimensional–unit hypersphere (a useful abstraction even if it cannot be visualized).

To train the Kohonen layer, an input vector is applied and its dot product is calculated with the weight vector associated with each Kohonen neuron. The neuron with the highest dot product is declared the "winner" and its weights are adjusted. Because the dot product operation used to calculate the NET values is a measure of similarity between the input and weight vectors, the training process actually consists of selecting the Kohonen neuron whose weight vector is most similar to the input vector, and making it still more similar. Note again that this is unsupervised training; there is

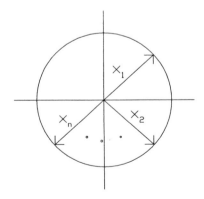

Figure 4-2b. Two-Dimensional Unit Vectors on the Unit Circle

no teacher. The network self-organizes so that a given Kohonen neuron has maximum output for a given input vector. The training equation that follows is used:

$$w_{new} = w_{old} + \alpha(x - w_{old}) \qquad (4\text{-}7)$$

where

w_{new} = the new value of a weight connecting an input component x to the winning neuron

w_{old} = the previous value of this weight

α = a training rate coefficient that may vary during the training process.

Each weight associated with the winning Kohonen neuron is changed by an amount proportional to the difference between its value and the value of the input to which it connects. The direction of the change minimizes the difference between the weight and its input.

Figure 4-3 shows this process geometrically in two-dimensional form. First, the vector $\mathbf{X} - \mathbf{W}_{old}$ is found by constructing a vector from the end of $\mathbf{W}$ to the end of $\mathbf{X}$. Next, this vector is shortened by multiplying it by the scalar α, a number less than one, thereby producing the change vector δ. Finally, the new weight vector $\mathbf{W}_{new}$ is a line from the origin to the end of δ. From this it may be seen that the effect of training is to rotate the weight vector toward the input vector without materially changing its length.

The variable α is a training-rate coefficient that usually starts out at about 0.7 and may be gradually reduced during training. This allows large initial steps for rapid, coarse training and smaller steps as the final value is approached.

If only one input vector were to be associated with each Kohonen neuron, the Kohonen layer could be trained with a single calculation per weight. The weights of a winning neuron would be made equal to the components of the training vector ($\alpha = 1$). Usually the training set includes many input vectors that are similar and the network should be trained to activate the same Kohonen neuron for each of them. In this case, the weights of that neuron should be the average of the input vectors that will activate it. Setting α to a low value will reduce the effect of each training step,

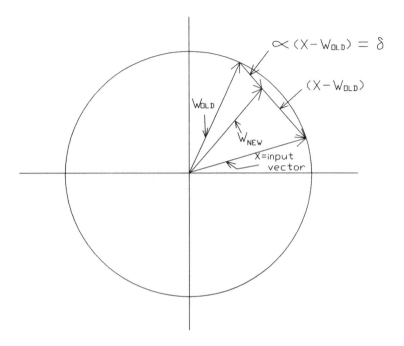

Figure 4-3. Rotating Weight Vector by Training

making the final value an average of the input vectors to which it was trained. In this way, the weights associated with a neuron will assume a value near the "center" of the input vectors for which that neuron is the "winner."

Initializing the Weight Vectors

All of the network weights must be set to initial values before training starts. It is common practice with neural networks to randomize the weights to small numbers. For Kohonen training, randomized weight vectors should be normalized. After training, the weight vectors must end up equal to normalized input vectors. Therefore, prenormalization to unit vectors will start weight vectors closer to their final state and thereby shorten the training process.

Randomizing the Kohonen layer weights can cause serious training problems, as it will uniformly distribute the weight vectors
around the hypersphere. Because the input vectors are usually not
evenly distributed and tend to be grouped on a relatively small
portion of the hypersphere surface, most of the weight vectors
will be so far away from any input vector that they will never be
the best match. These Kohonen neurons will always have an output of zero and will be wasted. Furthermore, the remaining
weights that do become the best match may be too few in number
to allow separation of input vector categories that are close together on the surface of the hypersphere.

Suppose there are several sets of input vectors all of which are
similar, yet must be separated into different categories. The network should be trained to activate a different Kohonen neuron for
each category. If the initial density of weight vectors is too low in
the vicinity of the training vectors, it may be impossible to separate
similar categories; there may not be enough weight vectors in the
vicinity to assign one to each input vector category.

Conversely, if several input vectors are slight variations of the
same pattern and should be lumped together, they should fire a
single Kohonen neuron. If the density of weight vectors is very
high near a group of slightly different input vectors, each input
vector may activate a different Kohonen neuron. This is not cata-
strophic, as the Grossberg layer can map different Kohonen neurons into the same output, but it is wasteful of Kohonen neurons.

The most desirable solution is to distribute the weight vectors
according to the density of input vectors that must be separated,
thereby placing more weight vectors in the vicinity of large-num-
ber input vectors. This is impractical to implement directly, but
several techniques approximate its effect.

One solution, called the *convex combination method*, sets all
the weights to the same value $1/\sqrt{(n)}$, where n is the number of
inputs and hence, the number of components in each weight vector. This makes the weight vectors of unit length and all coincident. Also, each component x_i of the input is given the value $\alpha x_i +$
$\{[1/\sqrt{(n)}] (1 - \alpha)\}$, where n is the number of inputs. Initially α is
given a very small value, causing all input vectors to have a length
near $1/\sqrt{(n)}$ and coincident with the weight vectors. As the network
trains, α is gradually increased to a limit of 1. This allows the input

vectors to separate and eventually assume their true values. The weight vectors follow one or a small group of input vectors and end the training process by producing the desired pattern of outputs. The convex combination method operates well but slows the training process, as the weight vectors are adjusting to a moving target. Another method adds noise to the input vectors. This causes them to move randomly, eventually capturing a weight vector. This method also works, but it is even slower than convex combination.

A third method starts with randomized weights but in the initial stages of the training process adjusts all of the weights, not just those associated with the winning Kohonen neuron. This moves the weight vectors around to the region of the input vectors. As training progresses, weight adjustments are restricted to those Kohonen neurons that are nearest to the winner. This radius of adjustment is gradually decreased until only those weights are adjusted that are associated with the winning Kohonen neuron.

Still another method (DeSieno 1988) gives each Kohonen neuron a "conscience." If it has been winning more than its fair share of the time (roughly $1/k$, where k is the number of Kohonen neurons), it temporarily raises a threshold that reduces its chances of winning, thereby allowing the other neurons an opportunity to be trained.

In many applications, the problem of weight distribution can seriously affect the accuracy of the result. Unfortunately, the effectiveness of the various solutions has not been fully evaluated and is certainly problem dependent.

Interpolative Mode

Up until this point we have been discussing a training algorithm in which only one Kohonen neuron is activated for each input vector; this is called the *accretive mode*. The accuracy of this method is limited in that the output is wholly a function of a single Kohonen neuron.

In the *interpolative mode*, a group of the Kohonen neurons having the highest outputs is allowed to present its outputs to the Grossberg layer. The number of neurons in this group must be chosen for the application, and there is no conclusive evidence regarding an optimum size. Once the group is determined, its set of NET outputs is treated as a vector and normalized to unit length by dividing each NET value by the square root of the sum of the squares of the NET values in the group. All neurons not in the group have their outputs set to zero.

The interpolative mode is capable of representing more complex mappings and can produce more accurate results. Again, no conclusive evidence is available to evaluate the interpolative versus the accretive modes.

Statistical Properties of the Trained Network

Kohonen training has the useful and interesting ability to extract the statistical properties of the input data set. Kohonen (1988) has shown that, in a fully trained network, the probability of a randomly selected input vector (selected according to the probability density function of the input set) being closest to any given weight vector is $1/k$, where k is the number of Kohonen neurons. This is the optimal distribution of weights on the hypersphere. (This assumes that all of the weight vectors are in use, a situation that will be realized only if one of the methods discussed is used to distribute the weight vectors.)

TRAINING THE GROSSBERG LAYER

The Grossberg layer is relatively simple to train. An input vector is applied, the Kohonen output(s) are established, and the Grossberg outputs are calculated as in normal operation. Next, each weight is adjusted only if it connects to a Kohonen neuron having a nonzero output. The amount of the weight adjustment is proportional to the difference between the weight and the desired output of the Grossberg neuron to which it connects. In symbols

$$v_{ij\ \text{new}} = v_{ij\ \text{old}} + \beta\ (y_j - v_{ij\ \text{old}})\ k_i \qquad (4\text{-}8)$$

where
  k_i = the output of Kohonen neuron i (only one Kohonen neuron is nonzero)

y_j = component j of the vector of desired outputs

Initially β is set to approximately 0.1 and is gradually reduced as training progresses.

From this it may be seen that the weights of the Grossberg layer will converge to the average values of the desired outputs, whereas the weights of the Kohonen layer are trained to the average values of the inputs. Grossberg training is supervised; the algorithm has a desired output to which it trains. The unsupervised, self-organizing operation of the Kohonen layer produces outputs at indeterminate positions; these are mapped to the desired outputs by the Grossberg layer.

THE FULL COUNTERPROPAGATION NETWORK

Figure 4-4 shows the full counterpropagation network. In normal operation, input vectors **X** and **Y** are applied and the trained network produces output vectors **X'** and **Y'**, which are approximations of **X** and **Y**, respectively. In this case, **X** and **Y** are assumed to

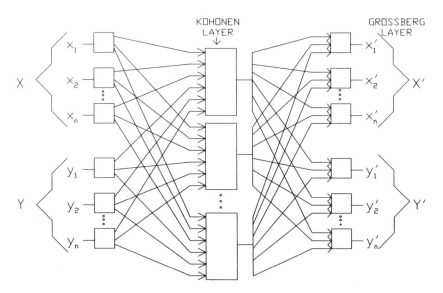

Figure 4-4. Full Counterpropagation Network

be normalized unit vectors; hence, they will tend to produce normalized vectors on the output.

During training, vectors **X** and **Y** are applied both as inputs to the network and as desired outputs. **X** is used to train the **X'** outputs, while **Y** is used to train the **Y'** outputs of the Grossberg layer. The full counterpropagation network is trained using the same method described for the feedforward network. The Kohonen neurons receive inputs from both the **X** and **Y** vectors, but these are indistinguishable from a single larger vector composed of the **X** and **Y** vectors; thus, this arrangement does not affect the training algorithm.

The result is an identity mapping in which the application of a pair of input vectors produces their replicas on the output. This does not seem very interesting until one realizes that applying only the **X** vector (with the **Y** vector set to 0) produces both the **X'** and **Y'** outputs. If F is a function mapping **X** to **Y'**, then the network approximates it. Also, if the inverse of F exists, applying only the **Y** vector (setting **X** to 0) produces **X'**. This unique ability to generate a function and its inverse makes the counterpropagation network useful in a number of applications.

Figure 4-4, unlike Hecht-Nielsen's original configuration (1987a), does not make apparent the counterflow nature of the network for which it is named. This form was chosen because it also illustrates the feedforward network and facilitates the extension of concepts developed in earlier chapters.

AN APPLICATION: DATA COMPRESSION

In addition to the usual vector-mapping functions, counterpropagation is useful in certain less obvious applications. One of the more interesting examples is data compression.

A counterpropagation network can be used to compress data prior to transmission, thereby reducing the number of bits that must be sent. Suppose that an image is to be transmitted. It can be divided into subimages **S** as shown in Figure 4-5. Each subimage is further divided into pixels (picture elements). Each subimage is then a vector, the elements of which are the pixels of which the subimage is composed. For simplicity, assume that each pixel is either one (light) or zero (dark). If there are n pixels in a subimage, then n bits will be required to transmit it. If some distortion can be

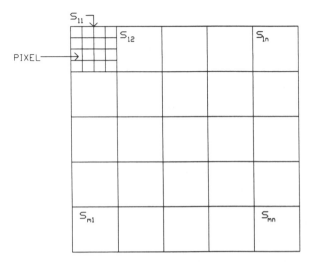

Figure 4-5. Image-Compression System

tolerated, substantially fewer bits are actually required to transmit typical images, thereby allowing an image to be transmitted more rapidly. This is possible because of the statistical distribution of subimage vectors; some occur frequently, while others occur so seldom that they can be approximated roughly. The method of *vector quantization* finds these shorter bit strings that best represent the subimages.

A counterpropagation network can be used to perform vector quantization. The set of subimage vectors is used as input to train the Kohonen layer in the accretive mode in which only a single neuron is allowed to be 1. The Grossberg layer weights are trained to produce the binary code of the index of the Kohonen neuron that is 1. For example, if Kohonen neuron 7 is 1 (and the others are all 0), the Grossberg layer will be trained to output 00 . . . 000111 (the binary code for 7). It is this shorter bit string that is transmitted.

At the receiving end, an identically trained counterpropagation network accepts the binary code and produces the inverse function, an approximation of the original subimage.

This method has been applied both to speech and images, yielding data compression ratios of 10:1 to 100:1. The quality has been acceptable, however some distortion of the data at the receiving end is inevitable.

DISCUSSION

Robert Hecht-Nielsen, the inventor of the counterpropagation network (CPN), realized its limitations: "CPN is obviously inferior to backpropagation for most mapping network applications. Its advantages are that it is simple and that it forms a good statistical model of its input vector environment" (1987a, p. 27).

It should be added that the counterpropagation network trains rapidly; appropriately applied it can save large amounts of computer time. It is also useful for rapid prototyping of systems, where the greater accuracy of backpropagation makes it the method of choice in the final version, but where a quick approximation is important. Also, the capability of generating a function and its inverse has found application in a number of systems.

References

DeSieno, D. 1988. Adding a conscience to competitive learning. *Proceedings of the IEEE International Conference on Neural Networks*, pp. 117–24. San Diego, CA: SOS Printing.

Grossberg, S. 1969. Some networks that can learn, remember and reproduce any number of complicated space-time patterns. *Journal of Mathematics and Mechanics* 19:53–91.

———. 1971. Embedding fields: Underlying philosophy, mathematics, and applications of psychology, physiology, and anatomy. *Journal of Cybernetics* 1:28–50.

———. 1982. *Studies of mind and brain*. Boston: Reidel.

Hecht-Nielsen, R. 1987a. Counterpropagation networks. In *Proceedings of the IEEE First International Conference on Neural Networks*, eds. M. Caudill and C. Butler, vol. 2, pp. 19–32. San Diego, CA: SOS Printing.

———. 1987b. Counterpropagation networks. *Applied Optics* 26(23): 4979–84.

———. 1988. Applications of counterpropagation networks. *Neural Networks* 1:131–39.

Kohonen, T. 1988. *Self-organization and associative memory*. 2d ed. New York: Springer-Verlag.

5

Statistical Methods

Statistical methods are useful both for training artificial neural networks and for producing the output from a previously trained network. Statistical training methods offer important advantages by avoiding local minima in the training process. But they create certain problems of their own.

Using statistical methods to produce the output from a network that has been previously trained is covered well by Hinton and Sejnowski (1986) and is discussed in Chapter 6; this chapter concentrates on network training.

TRAINING APPLICATIONS

An artificial neural network is trained by means of some process that modifies its weights. If the training is successful, application of a set of inputs to the network produces the desired set of outputs. There are two categories of training methods: deterministic and statistical. A *deterministic training method* follows a step-by-step procedure to adjust the network weights based upon their current values and the values of the inputs, actual outputs, and desired outputs. Perceptron training is an example of the deterministic approach (see Chapter 2).

Statistical training methods make pseudorandom changes in the weight values, retaining those changes that result in improvements. To see how this might be done, consider Figure 5-1, which shows a typical network in which neurons are connected by weights. Here, the output of a neuron is the weighted sum of its inputs, operated upon by some nonlinear function (see Chapter 2 for details). The following procedure can be used to train the network:

1. Apply a set of inputs and compute the resulting outputs.
2. Compare these outputs with the desired outputs and calculate a measure of their difference. A commonly used method finds the difference between the actual and desired outputs of each element of a training pair, squares the differences, and sums all of the squares. The object of training is to minimize this difference, often called the *objective function*.
3. Select a weight at random and adjust it by a small random amount. If the adjustment helps (reduces the objective function), retain it; otherwise, return the weight to its previous value.
4. Repeat steps 1 through 3 until the network is trained to the desired degree.

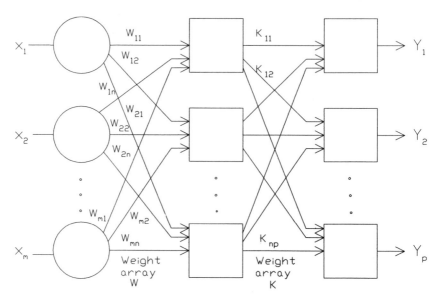

Figure 5-1. Two-Layer Feedforward Network

This process tends to minimize the objective function but can get trapped in a poor solution. Figure 5-2 shows how this can occur in a system with a single weight. Assume the weight is set initially to the value at point A. If the random weight steps are small, all deviations from point A increase the objective function and will be rejected. The superior weight setting at point B will never be found and the system will be trapped in a "local minimum" instead of the "global minimum" at point B. If the random weight adjustments are very large, both point A and point B will be visited frequently, but so will every other point. The weight will change so drastically that it will never settle into the desired minimum.

A useful strategy to avoid these problems starts with large steps and gradually reduces the size of the average random step. This allows the network to escape local minima, while ensuring eventual network stabilization.

Local minimum entrapment plagues all "minimum-seeking" training algorithms. This includes perceptron and backpropagation networks and represents a serious and widespread difficulty that is often overlooked. Statistical methods can overcome this problem; a weight adjustment strategy that causes the weights to assume the globally optimal value of point B is possible.

As an explanatory analogy, suppose that Figure 5-2 represents a marble on a surface in a box. If the box is shaken violently in a horizontal direction, the marble will move rapidly from side to

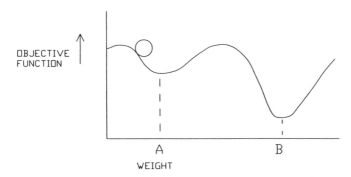

Figure 5-2. Local-Minimum Problem

side. Never settling at one point, at any instant the marble may be at any point on the surface with equal probability.

If the violence of the shaking is gradually reduced, a condition will be reached in which the marble "sticks" briefly at point B. At a still lower level of shaking, the marble will stay at both points A and B for short times. If the shaking is continually reduced, a critical point will be reached where the shaking is just strong enough to move the marble from point A to B, but not strong enough to enable the marble to climb the hill from B to A. Thus, the marble will end up in a global minimum as the shaking amplitude is reduced to zero.

Artificial neural networks can be trained in essentially the same way through random adjustments of weights. At first, large random adjustments are made, retaining only those weight changes that reduce the objective function. The average step size is then gradually reduced and a global minimum will eventually be reached.

This procedure has a strong resemblance to the annealing of metals; hence, the term "simulated annealing" is often used to describe it. In a metal raised to a temperature above its melting point, the atoms are in violent random motion. As with all physical systems, the atoms tend toward minimum energy state (a single crystal in this case), but at high temperatures the vigor of the atomic motions prevents this. As the metal is gradually cooled, lower and lower energy states are assumed until finally the lowest of all possible states, a global minimum, is achieved. In the annealing process, the distribution of energy states is determined by the relationship that follows:

$$P(e) \propto \exp\left(-e/kT\right) \tag{5-1}$$

where
  $P(e)$ = the probability that the system is in a state with energy e
  k = Boltzmann's constant
  T = temperature, degrees Kelvin

At high temperatures $P(e)$ approaches one for all energy states. Thus, a high energy state is almost as likely as a low energy state. As the temperature is reduced, the probability of high energy states decreases as compared to the probability of low energy states. As the temperature approaches zero, it becomes very unlikely that the system will exist in a high energy state.

Boltzmann Training

Applying this statistical method to the training of artificial neural networks is straightforward:

1. Define a variable T that represents an artificial temperature. Start with T at a large value.
2. Apply a set of inputs to the network, and calculate the outputs and objective function.
3. Make a random weight change, and recalculate the network output and the change in objective function due to the weight change.
4. If the objective function is reduced (improved), retain the weight change.

If the weight change results in an increase in the objective function, calculate the probability of accepting that change from the Boltzmann distribution as follows:

$$P(c) = \exp\left(-c/kT\right) \qquad (5\text{-}2)$$

where
   $P(c)$ = the probability of a change of c in the objective function
   k = a constant analogous to Boltzmann's constant that must be chosen for the problem at hand
   T = the artificial temperature

Select a random number r from a uniform distribution between zero and one. If $P(c)$ is greater than r, retain the change; otherwise, return the weight to the previous value.

This allows the system to take an occasional step in a direction that worsens the objective function, thereby permitting it to escape a local minimum where any small step raises the objective function.

To complete the Boltzmann training strategy, repeat steps 3 and 4 over *each* of the weights in the network, gradually reducing the temperature T until an acceptably low value for the objective function is achieved. At this point, a different input vector is applied and the training process is repeated. The network is trained on all vectors in the training set, perhaps repeatedly, until the objective function is acceptable for each.

The size of the random weight change in step 3 can be determined in many ways. For example, emulating the thermal system, the weight change w can be selected according to the Gaussian distribution:

$$P(w) = \exp\left(-w^2/T^2\right) \tag{5-3}$$

where
    $P(w)$ = the probability of a weight change of size w
    T = the artificial temperature

This weight-change selection method produces a system analogous to the method described by Metropolis et al. (1953).

Because the value of the weight change Δw is desired rather than the probability of a weight change of size w, the Monte Carlo method can be used as follows to produce the needed result:

1. Find the cumulative probability function corresponding to $P(w)$. This is the integral of $P(w)$ from 0 to w. Because in this case $P(w)$ cannot be integrated by ordinary methods, it must be integrated numerically and the result tabulated as Δw.
2. Select a random number from a uniform distribution over the interval . Use this as a value for $P(w)$ and look up the corresponding value for Δw.

The characteristics of the Boltzmann machine have been studied extensively. Geman and Geman (1984) proved that the rate of temperature reduction must be proportional to the reciprocal logarithm of time, if convergence to a global minimum is to be achieved. The cooling rate in this system is expressed as follows:

$$T(t) = T_0/\log\left(1 + t\right) \tag{5-4}$$

where

$T(t)$ = artificial temperature as a function of time
T_0 = initial artificial temperature
t = artificial time

This discouraging result predicts very low cooling rates (and long computations). This conclusion has been borne out experimentally; Boltzmann machines often take impractical periods of time to train.

Cauchy Training

Szu and Hartley (1987) developed a method for rapid training of these systems. Their method substitutes the Cauchy distribution for the Boltzmann distribution when calculating the step size. As shown in Figure 5-3, the Cauchy distribution has longer "tails," thereby increasing the probability of large step sizes. In fact, the Cauchy distribution has infinite (undefined) variance. By this simple change, the maximum temperature reduction rate is made inversely linear rather than inversely logarithmic, as in the Boltzmann training algorithm. This drastically reduces the training time. This relationship can be expressed as follows:

$$T(t) = T_0/(1 + t) \tag{5-5}$$

The Cauchy distribution is

$$P(x) = T(t)/[T(t)^2 + x^2] \tag{5-6}$$

where $P(x)$ is the probability of a step of size x.

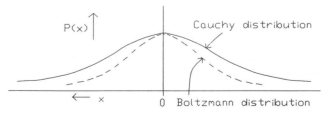

Figure 5-3. Cauchy versus Boltzmann Distributions

$P(x)$ can be integrated by usual methods. Then solving for x yields the expression

$$x_c = \rho\{T(t) \tan [P(x)]\} \qquad (5\text{-}7)$$

where

ρ = the learning rate coefficient

x_c = the weight change

The Monte Carlo method then becomes very simple. To find x in this case, select a random number from a uniform distribution over the open interval $(-\pi/2, \pi/2)$ (necessary to bound the tangent function). Substitute this for $P(x)$ and calculate the step size x using the current temperature.

Artificial Specific Heat Method

Despite the improvement of the Cauchy method, training times can still be long. A technique rooted in thermodynamics can been used to accelerate this process. This method involves adjusting the temperature-reduction rate according to an artificial "specific heat" calculated during the training process.

Phase changes occur during the annealing of a metal; these represent discrete energy levels. At each phase transition, there may be a rather abrupt change in a quantity termed specific heat. *Specific heat* is defined as the rate of change of temperature with energy; the changes in specific heat result from the system "settling" into one of the local energy minima.

Artificial neural networks pass through analogous phases during training. At the boundary of a phase change, the artificial specific heat may change abruptly. This pseudospecific heat is defined as the average of the rate of change of temperature with the objective function. As in the marble-in-a-box example, violent initial changes make the average value of the objective function virtually independent of small changes in temperature, so the specific heat is nearly constant. Also, at very low temperatures, the system is frozen into a minimum, so again the specific heat is nearly constant. Clearly, the temperature can be allowed to change rapidly in both of these ranges, as no improvement in the objective function is occurring.

At critical temperatures, a small temperature decrease causes a large decrease in the average value of the objective function. Returning to the marble analogy, at the "temperature" where the marble has just enough average energy to go from A to B, but not enough to go from B to A, the average value of the objective function makes an abrupt change. At these critical points, the algorithm must change the temperature very slowly to ensure that the system does not accidentally get frozen at point A, thereby becoming trapped at a local minimum. The critical temperatures can be detected as abrupt decreases in the artificial specific heat, that is, the average of the rate of change of temperature with the objective function. Once a critical temperature has been reached, temperatures close to this value must be traversed slowly to ensure convergence to a global minimum. At all other temperatures, a higher rate of temperature reduction can be safely used, thereby producing a significant reduction in training time.

APPLICATIONS TO GENERAL NONLINEAR OPTIMIZATION PROBLEMS

The discussion up to this point has assumed that we are adjusting weights in a traditional artificial neural network. In fact, however, this is a special case; these statistical techniques are far more general and are capable of solving a variety of problems in nonlinear optimization.

A *nonlinear optimization problem* involves a set of independent variables that are related to the value of an objective function in a deterministic fashion. The goal is to find the set of values for the independent variables that minimizes (or maximizes) the objective function. For example, consider finding the minimum of the function $F(x) = 3x^3 + 5x^2 - 2x + 3$.

Here, there is a single independent variable x that controls the value of the objective function $F(x)$, which is to be minimized. The Cauchy technique previously used for training a network can be used to select a value for x that minimizes $F(x)$. This simple function is easily minimized using differential calculus; however, more complicated functions of a large number of variables can be prohibitively difficult to minimize in this way.

In many practical situations, the functional relationship between the independent variables and the objective function is unknown and, in a practical sense, unknowable. A complex chemical process may have no adequate mathematical model. The only measurable quantities may be "yield," "quality," "cost," and so on, which are some unknown function of a large number of such independent variables as temperature, time, and raw material characteristics.

Such a problem can be solved as follows:

1. Observe the system and collect data to make a training set. Each element of the training set consists of measurements from a specific observation and includes values for all inputs (the input vector) and for the outputs (the output vector).

2. Train the network over this training set. The training is accomplished by applying an input vector, computing the output vector, comparing the output vector to the observed output vector, and adjusting the weights to minimize the difference. Each input vector is applied in turn and the network is partially trained. After a large number of applications of the input vectors, the network will converge to a solution that minimizes the difference between the desired and measured system outputs.

In effect, the network constructs an internal model of an unknown system. If the training set is large enough, the network converges to an accurate model of the system. If the network is presented with an input vector different from any vector applied during training, a perfectly trained network will produce the same output vector as the actual system would.

3. Maximize the objective function. An objective function of the outputs must be devised to represent the degree of "goodness" of the result. At this point, the inputs become the variables to the trained network. They are adjusted using the same training algorithm used to set the weights in step 2; however, inputs are now used to maximize the objective function.

In many cases, there may be constraints imposed by the problem. For example, it may not be physically possible to achieve values of the variables outside of a specified range. These constraints (which may be complicated expressions) are easily accommodated by rejecting any input variable change in step 3 that violates a constraint.

This generalization of the stochastic optimization technique makes the method applicable to a wide range of optimization problems. Other training methods can also be applied, but the stochastic technique overcomes the difficulty of local minima solutions that are inherent to backpropagation and other gradient-descent methods. Unfortunately, the random nature of the training process can result in long convergence times. Using pseudospecific heat methods can reduce this time considerably, but the process remains inherently slow.

BACKPROPAGATION AND CAUCHY TRAINING: AN OVERVIEW

Backpropagation has the advantage of a directed search; that is, the weights are always adjusted in the direction that minimizes the error function. While the training time is often lengthy, it is considerably faster than the random-search method of the Cauchy machine, which finds a global minimum, but may take many incorrect steps and a long time in the process.

Combining the two techniques has produced encouraging results (Wasserman 1988). Making the weight adjustment equal to the sum of that calculated by the backpropagation algorithm and the random step required by the Cauchy algorithm produces a system that converges and finds the global minimum more rapidly than a system trained by either method alone. A simple heuristic is used to avoid network paralysis, a problem that can occur in either backpropagation or Cauchy training procedures.

Problems with Backpropagation

Despite the demonstrated power of backpropagation, several problems plague its application, although some of these have been alleviated through the use of a new algorithm.

Convergence

Rumelhart, Hinton, and Williams (1986) provide a convergence proof cast in terms of partial differential equations—making it valid only if network weights are adjusted in infinitesimal steps. Because this implies infinite convergence time, it proves nothing about training times in practical applications. In fact, there is no proof that backpropagation will ever converge with a finite step size. Empirical observations show that networks usually train, but the duration of the training process is unpredictable and lengthy.

Local Minima

Backpropagation uses gradient descent to adjust the network weights, following the local slope of the error surface toward a minimum. This works well with convex error surfaces, which have a unique minimum, but it often leads to nonoptimal solutions with the highly convoluted, nonconvex surfaces encountered in practical problems. In some cases, a local minimum is an acceptable solution; in others, it is inadequate.

Even after the network has trained, there is no way to tell if backpropagation has found the global minimum. If a solution is not satisfactory, one is obliged to initialize the weights to new random values and to retrain the network, with no guarantee that it will train on a given trial or that a global minimum will ever be found.

Paralysis

Under some circumstances, a network can train itself into a state in which weight modification comes to a virtual standstill. This "network paralysis" is a serious problem; once entered, it can extend training time by orders of magnitude.

Paralysis occurs when a large percentage of the neurons have acquired weights so large as to produce high values for NET. This causes OUT to approach its limit; at these points the derivative of the squashing function approaches zero. As we have seen, the backpropagation algorithm calculates the magnitude of the weight change using this derivative as a factor in the expression. For affected neurons, the near-zero derivative causes the weight change to approach zero; if the condition is widespread throughout the network, training can slow to a near halt.

There is no theory that predicts whether or not a network will become paralyzed during training. Experimentally, small step sizes have been found to produce paralysis less often, but a step that is small for one problem may be excessive for another. The cost of paralysis can be high. Simulations can consume many hours of computer time, only to end in a paralytic training failure.

Problems with the Cauchy Training Algorithm

Despite the improvement in training rate provided by the Cauchy machine as compared to the Boltzmann machine, convergence times can still be 100 times those of the backpropagation algorithm. Also, network paralysis is particularly severe using the Cauchy training algorithm, especially in a network with nonlinearity, such as the logistic function. The infinite variance of the Cauchy distribution allows weight changes of unlimited magnitude. Furthermore, large weight changes will sometimes be accepted even though they are disadvantageous, often resulting in severe saturation of neurons in the network, with the resulting risk of paralysis.

Combined Backpropagation/Cauchy Training

Weight adjustments in the combined backpropagation/Cauchy algorithm consist of two components: (1) a directed component, calculated using the backpropagation algorithm; and (2) a random component, determined by the Cauchy distribution.

These components are calculated for each weight and their sum is the amount by which the weight is changed. As in the Cauchy algorithm, the objective function is calculated after a weight change. If there is an improvement, the change is retained; otherwise, it is retained with a probability determined by the Boltzmann distribution.

The weight adjustment is calculated using the equations for the two algorithms presented previously:

$$w_{mn,k}(n + 1) = w_{mn,k}(n) + \eta \left[\alpha \Delta w_{mn,k}(n) + (1 - \alpha) \delta_{n,k} \, \mathrm{OUT}_{m,j} \right] + (1 - \eta) x_c$$

where η is a coefficient controlling the relative magnitudes of the Cauchy and backpropagation components of the weight step. If η is set to zero, the system becomes a pure Cauchy machine; if η is set to one, it becomes a backpropagation machine.

Changing only one weight between calculations of the objective function is computationally inefficient; it has been found that changing all of the weights of a layer is a better compromise, although some problems may require another strategy.

Overcoming Network Paralysis with
Combined-Method Training

As with the pure Cauchy machine, if a weight change worsens the objective function, the Boltzmann distribution is used to decide if the new weight value should be retained, or the previous value restored. Thus, there is a finite probability that a disastrous set of weight changes may be retained. Since the Cauchy distribution has infinite variance (the range of the tangent function spans $-\infty$ to $+\infty$ over the specified domain), it is quite capable of producing tremendous weight changes, often leading to network paralysis.

The obvious solution of limiting the range of the weight steps creates questions about the mathematical soundness of the resulting algorithm. Szu and Hartley (1987) have proven that the system converges to a global minimum at an excellent rate if the algorithm is left intact; no such proof exists if the step size is artificially limited. In fact, experiments have shown cases in which large weights are required to implement a function, as when two large weights must be subtracted to produce a small difference.

Another solution randomizes the weights of neurons that are found to be in saturation. This is disadvantageous in that it can badly disrupt the training process, sometimes prolonging it indefinitely.

A method has been found to solve the paralysis problem while leaving previous training nearly intact. Here, saturated neurons are detected by inspecting their OUT signals. If the magnitude of OUT is approaching the limiting value, either positive or negative, all of the weights feeding that neuron are operated upon by a squashing function, much like that used to produce the OUT signal of the neuron, except that the range of the function is set to $(+5, -5)$, or some other suitable value. The modified weight values are then

$$w_{mn} = -5 + 10/[1 + \exp(-w_{mn}/5)]$$

This function severely reduces the magnitude of excessively large weights; small weights are much less affected. Furthermore, it maintains symmetry, thereby preserving small differences between large weights. It has been shown experimentally that the function pulls neurons out of saturation, without excessive disturbance of the existing network training. There has been no major effort made to optimize this function; other values of the constants may prove superior.

Experimental Results

The new backpropagation/Cauchy algorithm has been used to train several large networks. For example, the handwritten Chinese character recognition system, reported in Wasserman (1988), was successfully trained using this method. Still, training times can be long (an average of 36 hours of computer time was required for this training task).

In another experiment, this network was trained on the exclusive-or problem to produce a training test that could be compared to the work of others. An average of 76 presentations of the training set was required for the network to converge. This may be compared to the average of 245 presentations reported by Rumelhart, Hinton, and Williams (1986) using backpropagation, and the 4,986 iterations reported by Parker (1987) with second-order backpropagation, both solving the exclusive-or problem.

No training session resulted in a local minimum, such as Rumelhart found in his work on this problem. Furthermore, the 160 training sessions disclosed no unexpected pathologies; the network always trained correctly.

Experiments with the Cauchy machine alone produced much longer training times. For example, at $\rho = .002$ an average of 2,284 presentations of the training set were required to train the network.

Discussion

The combined backpropagation/Cauchy network trains significantly faster than either algorithm alone, and is relatively insensitive to the values of the coefficients. Convergence to a global minimum is guaranteed by the Cauchy algorithm; hundreds of training experiments have produced no case in which the network became trapped in a local minimum. Network paralysis has been solved by the use of a selective weight-compression algorithm that has produced convergence in all tests to date, without materially increasing training time.

Despite these encouraging results, the method is not fully evaluated, especially on large problems. Much more work will be required to determine its advantages and disadvantages.

References

Geman, S., and Geman, D. 1984. Stochastic relaxation, Gibbs distributions and Baysian restoration of images. *IEEE Transactions on Pattern Analysis and Machine Intelligence* 6:721–41.

Hinton, G.E., and Sejnowski, T. J. 1986. Learning and relearning in Boltzmann machines. In *Parallel distributed processing*, vol.1, pp. 282–317. Cambridge, MA: MIT Press.

Metropolis, N., Rosenbluth, A. W., Rosenbluth, M. N., Teller, A. H., and Teller, E. 1953. Equations of state calculations by fast computing machines. *Journal of Chemistry and Physics* 21:1087–91.

Parker, D. B. 1987. Optimal algorithms for adaptive networks: Second order backpropagation, second order direct propagation, and second order Hebbian learning. In *Proceedings of the IEEE First International Conference on Neural Networks*, eds. M. Caudill and C. Butler, vol. 2, pp. 593–600. San Diego, CA: SOS Printing.

Rumelhart, D. E., Hinton, G. E., and Williams, R. J. 1986. Learning internal representations by error propagation. In *Parallel distributed processing*, vol.1, pp. 318–62. Cambridge, MA: MIT Press.

Szu, H., and Hartley, R. 1987. Fast simulated annealing. *Physics Letters* 1222(3,4):157–62.

Wasserman, P. D. 1988. Combined backpropagation/Cauchy machine. *Neural Networks: Abstracts of the First INNS Meeting, Boston 1988*, vol. 1, p. 556. Elmsford, NY: Pergamon Press.

6

Hopfield Nets

The networks presented in previous chapters are nonrecurrent; that is, there is no feedback from the outputs of the networks to their inputs. The lack of feedback ensures that the networks are unconditionally stable. They cannot enter a mode in which the output wanders interminably from state to state, never producing a usable output. This highly desirable characteristic comes with a price; nonrecurrent networks have a repertoire of behavior that is limited compared to their recurrent kin.

Because recurrent networks have feedback paths from their outputs back to their inputs, the response of such networks is dynamic; that is, after applying a new input, the output is calculated and fed back to modify the input. The output is then recalculated, and the process is repeated again and again. For a stable network, successive iterations produce smaller and smaller output changes until eventually the outputs become constant. For many networks, the process never ends, and such networks are said to be unstable. Unstable networks have interesting properties and have been studied as examples of chaotic systems. The large subject of chaos is outside of the scope of this volume, however. Instead, we concentrate on stable networks, that is, those that eventually produce a constant output.

Stability problems stymied early researchers. No one was able to predict which networks would be stable and which would change continuously. Furthermore, the problem appeared so difficult that many researchers were pessimistic about finding a solution. Fortunately, a powerful network theorem that defines a subset of the recurrent networks whose outputs eventually reach a stable state has been devised (Cohen and Grossberg 1983). This brilliant accomplishment opened the door to further research, and today many scientists are exploring the complicated behavior and capabilities of these systems.

John Hopfield has made important contributions to both the theory and application of recurrent systems. As a result, some configurations have become known as Hopfield nets. A review of the literature shows that many others have conducted research on these and similar devices; for example, Grossberg (1987) has studied the general properties of networks similar to many of those presented here. The works cited at the end of this chapter are not intended to constitute an exhaustive list of titles on the subject of recurrent systems; rather they are accessible writings that can serve to explain, amplify, and extend the contents of this volume.

RECURRENT NETWORK CONFIGURATIONS

Figure 6-1 shows a recurrent network consisting of two layers. The format is somewhat different from that found in the work of Hopfield and others, however, it is functionally equivalent and ties in well with the networks presented in earlier chapters. Layer 0, as in previous illustrations, serves no computational function; it simply distributes the network outputs back to the inputs. Each layer 1 neuron computes the weighted sum of its inputs, producing a NET signal that is then operated on by the nonlinear function F to yield the OUT signal. These operations are similar to the neurons of other networks (see Chapter 2).

Binary Systems

In Hopfield's early work (1982), the function F was a simple threshold. The output of such a neuron is one if the weighted sum of the outputs of the other neurons is greater than a threshold T_j; otherwise it is 0. It is calculated as follows:

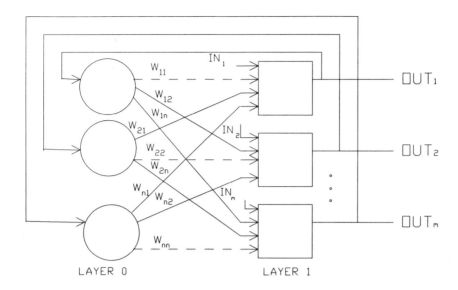

dotted lines indicate weights of zero

Figure 6-1. Single-Layer Recurrent Network

$$\text{NET}_j = \sum_{i \neq j} w_{ij}\text{OUT}_i + \text{IN}_j \qquad (6\text{-}1)$$

$\text{OUT}_j = 1$ if $\text{NET}_j > T_j$

$\text{OUT}_j = 0$ if $\text{NET}_j < T_j$

OUT_j unchanged if $\text{NET}_j = T_j$

The *state of a network* is simply the set of the current values of the OUT signals from all neurons. In the original Hopfield network, the state of each neuron changed at discrete random times; in later work, the neuron states could change simultaneously. Because the output of a binary neuron can be only one or zero (intermediate levels are not allowed), the current state of the network forms a binary number, each bit of which represents the OUT signal from a neuron.

The network's operation is easily visualized geometrically. Figure 6-2a shows the case for two neurons in the output layer in which each of the four system states (00, 01, 10, 11) labels a vertex

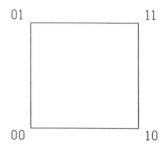

Figure 6-2a. Two Neurons Produce Four System States

of a square. Figure 6-2b shows a three-neuron system represented by a cube (in three-dimensional space) having eight vertexes, each labeled with a three-bit binary number. In general, a system with n neurons has 2^n distinct states and is associated with an n-dimensional hypercube.

When a new input vector is applied, the network moves from vertex to vertex until it stabilizes. The stable vertex is determined by the network weights, the current inputs, and the threshold value. If the input vector is partially incorrect or incomplete, the network stabilizes to the vertex closest to the one desired.

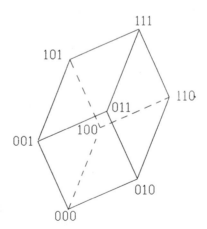

Figure 6-2b. Three Neurons Produce Eight System States

Stability

As with other networks, the weights between layers in this network may be considered to form a matrix **W**. Cohen and Grossberg (1983) have shown that recurrent networks are stable if the matrix is symmetrical with zeros on its main diagonal; that is, if $w_{ij} = w_{ji}$ for i not equal to j, and $w_{ii} = 0$ for all i.

The stability of such a network may be proven through an elegant mathematical technique. Suppose a function can be found that always decreases each time the network changes state. Eventually this function must reach a minimum and stop, thereby ensuring that the network is stable. The function that follows is called a Liapunov function and works in just such a manner on the recurrent networks presented above:

$$E = (-1/2) \sum_i \sum_j w_{ij} \, \text{OUT}_i \, \text{OUT}_j - \sum_j I_j \, \text{OUT}_j + \sum_j T_j \, \text{OUT}_j \quad (6\text{-}2)$$

where

$\quad E$ = an artificial network energy
$\quad w_{ij}$ = weight from the output of neuron i to the input of neuron j
$\quad \text{OUT}_j$ = output of neuron j
$\quad I_j$ = external input to neuron j
$\quad T_j$ = threshold of neuron j

The change in energy E, due to a change in the state of neuron j, is

$$\delta E = - \left[\sum_{i \neq j} (w_{ij} \, \text{OUT}_i) + I_j - T_j \right] \delta \, \text{OUT}_j$$

$$= - [\text{NET}_j - T_j] \, \delta \, \text{OUT}_j \quad (6\text{-}3)$$

where $\delta \, \text{OUT}_j$ is the change in the output of neuron j

Suppose that the NET value of neuron j is greater than the threshold. This will cause the term in brackets to be positive and, from Equation 6-1, the output of neuron j must change in the positive direction (or remain constant). This means that $\delta \, \text{OUT}_j$ can be only positive or zero, and δE must be negative; hence, the network energy must either decrease or stay constant.

Next, assume that NET is less than the threshold. Then $\delta \, \text{OUT}_j$

can be only negative or zero; hence, again the energy must decrease or stay constant.

Finally, if NET equals the threshold, δ_j is zero and the energy remains unchanged.

This shows that any change in the state of a neuron will either reduce the energy or maintain its current value. Because the energy shows this continuous downward trend, eventually it must find a minimum and stop. By definition, such a network is stable.

The network symmetry criterion is sufficient, but not necessary, to define a stable system. There are many stable systems (e.g., all feedforward networks!) that do not satisfy it. Also, examples can be shown in which minute deviations from symmetry can produce continuous oscillations; however, approximate symmetry is usually adequate to produce stable systems.

Associative Memory

Human memory operates in an associative manner; that is, a portion of a recollection can produce a larger related memory. For example, hearing only a few bars of music may recall a complete sensory experience, including scenes, sounds, and odors. By contrast, ordinary computer memory is location addressable; an address is applied and the data occupying that address is returned.

A recurrent network forms an associative memory. Like human memory, a portion of the desired data is supplied and the full data "memory" is returned. To make an associative memory using a recurrent network, the weights must be selected to produce energy minima at the desired vertexes of the unit hypercube.

Hopfield (1984) has developed an associative memory in which the outputs are continuous, ranging from $+1$ to -1, corresponding to the binary values 0 and 1, respectively. The memories are encoded as binary vectors and stored in the weights according to the formula that follows:

$$w_{ij} = \sum_{d = 1 \text{ to } m} (\text{OUT}_{i,d}\, \text{OUT}_{j,d}) \qquad (6\text{-}4)$$

where

    m = the number of desired memories (output vectors)

d = the number of a desired memory (output vector)
$\text{OUT}_{i,d}$ = the ith component of the desired output vector

This expression may be clarified by noting that the weight array **W** can be found by calculating the outer product of each desired vector with itself (if the desired vector has n components, this operation forms an n-by-n matrix) and summing all of the matrixes thus formed. This may be expressed symbolically as follows:

$$\mathbf{W} = \sum_i \mathbf{D}_i' \, \mathbf{D}_i \qquad (6\text{-}5)$$

where $\mathbf{D}_i$ is the ith desired row vector.

Once the weights are determined, the network may be used to produce the desired output vector, even given an input vector that may be partially incorrect or incomplete. To do so, the outputs of the network are first forced to the values of this input vector. Next, the input vector is removed and the network is allowed to "relax" toward the closest deep minimum. Note that the network follows the local slope of the energy function, and it may become trapped in a local minimum and not find the best solution in a global sense.

Continuous Systems

Hopfield (1984) shows other cases in which the activation function F is continuous, thereby more accurately simulating the biological neuron. A common choice is the S-shaped sigmoid or logistic function

$$F(x) = 1/(1 + e^{-\lambda \text{NET}}) \qquad (6\text{-}6)$$

where λ is a coefficient that determines the steepness of the sigmoidal function. If λ is large, F approaches the threshold function previously described; smaller values for λ produce a more gentle slope.

Like the binary system, stability is ensured if the weights are symmetrical; that is, $w_{ij} = w_{ji}$ and $w_{ii} = 0$ for all i. An energy function that proves such networks stable has been devised, but it is not treated here due to its conceptual similarity to the discrete case.

Interested readers should consult Cohen and Grossberg (1983) for a more complete treatment of this important topic.

If the value of λ is large, continuous systems perform much like discrete binary systems, ultimately stabilizing with all outputs near zero or one, a vertex of the unit hypercube. As λ is reduced, stable points move away from the vertexes, disappearing one by one as λ approaches zero. Figure 6-3 shows an energy contour map for a continuous system consisting of two neurons.

Hopfield Nets and the Boltzmann Machine

Hopfield nets suffer from a tendency to stabilize to a local rather than a global minimum of the energy function. This problem is largely solved by a class of networks known as Boltzmann machines, in which the neurons change state in a statistical rather than a deterministic fashion. There is a close analogy between these methods and the way in which a metal is annealed; hence, the methods are often called *simulated annealing.*

Figure 6-3. Energy Contour Map

Thermodynamic Systems

A metal is annealed by heating it to a temperature above its melting point, and then letting it cool gradually. At high temperatures, the atoms possess high energies and move about freely, randomly assuming every possible configuration. As temperature is gradually reduced, the atomic energies decrease and the system as a whole tends to settle into a minimum-energy configuration. Finally, when the cooling is complete, a state is reached where the system energy is at a global minimum.

At a given temperature, the probability distribution of system energies is determined by the Boltzmann probability factor

$$\exp\left(-E/kT\right)$$

where
  E = system energy
  k = Boltzmann's constant
  T = temperature

From this it may be seen that there is a finite probability of the system's possessing high energy even at low temperatures. Likewise, there is a small but calculable probability that a kettle of water on a fire will freeze before it boils.

The statistical distribution of energies allows the system to escape a local energy minimum. At the same time, the probability of high system energy decreases rapidly as temperature drops; hence, there is a strong bias toward low energy states at low temperatures.

Statistical Hopfield Networks

If the state-change rules for the binary Hopfield net are determined statistically rather than deterministically as in Equation 6-1, a simulated-annealing system results. To accomplish this, the probability of a weight change is determined by the amount by which the NET output of a neuron exceeds its threshold. In symbols, let

$$E_k = \text{NET}_k - \theta_k$$

where
   NET_k = the NET output of neuron k
   θ_k = the threshold of neuron k

and

$$p_k = 1/[1 + \exp(-\delta E_k/T)]$$

(note the Boltzmann probability function in the denominator)

where T is artificial temperature.

   In operation, the artificial temperature T is set to a high value, neurons are clamped to an initial state determined by an input vector, and the network is allowed to seek an energy minimum according to the procedure that follows:

1. For each neuron, set the state to one, with a probability equal to p_k; otherwise, set its state to zero.
2. Gradually reduce the artificial temperature and repeat step 1 until equilibrium is reached.

Generalized Networks

The Boltzmann-machine technique can be extended to networks of virtually any configuration, although stability cannot be guaranteed. To do so, simply select one set of neurons to serve as inputs and another set to serve as outputs. Clamp the input set to the values of the input vector and allow the network to relax according to steps 1 and 2 above.

   A training procedure for such a network has been described by Hinton and Sejnowski (1986), consisting of the steps that follow:

1. Calculate clamped probabilities.
   a. Clamp input and output neurons to the training vector values.
   b. Allow the network to find equilibrium.
   c. Record the output values for all units.
   d. Repeat steps a through c for all training vectors.
   e. Calculate $P^+{}_{ij}$, or the probability over all training vectors that unit i and unit j are both one.

2. Calculate unclamped probabilities.
   a. Starting from a random state, allow the network to "free run" with no inputs or outputs clamped.
   b. Repeat step 2a a large number of times, recording values of all neurons.
   c. Calculate P^-_{ij}, or the probability that units i and j are both one.
3. Adjust network weights as follows:

$$\delta w_{ij} = \eta \ [P^+_{ij} - P^-_{ij}]$$

where
δw_{ij} = the change in weight w_{ij}
η = the learning rate coefficient

APPLICATIONS

Analog-to-Digital Converter

In recent works (Hopfield and Tank 1985; Tank and Hopfield 1986), an electrical circuit has been presented that uses a recurrent network to produce a four-bit analog-to-digital converter. Figure 6-4 shows a block diagram of the circuit, with amplifiers serving as artificial neurons. Resistors, representing weights, connect each neuron's output to the inputs of all others. To satisfy the stability constraint, no resistor connects a neuron's output to its own input and the weights are symmetrical; that is, a resistor from the output of neuron i to the input of neuron j has the same value as the resistor from the output of neuron j to the input of neuron i.

Note that the amplifiers have both normal and inverting outputs. This takes into account the case in which a weight must be negative, while permitting the use of ordinary positive-valued resistors for all weights. All possible resistors are shown in Figure 6-4; however, in no case is it necessary to connect both the normal and inverted outputs of a neuron to another neuron's input.

In a realistic circuit, each amplifier will have a finite input resistance and input capacitance that must be included to characterize the dynamic response. Network stability does not require that these elements be the same for all amplifiers, nor need they be

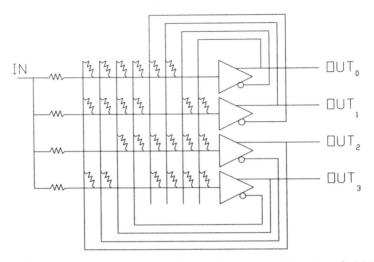

Figure 6-4. Four-Bit Analog-to-Digital Converter Using Hopfield Net

symmetrical. Because these elements affect only the time required to reach a solution and not the solution itself, they have been omitted to simplify the analysis.

The application assumes that a threshold function is used (the limit of the sigmoid function as λ approaches ∞). Furthermore, all of the outputs are changed at the beginning of discrete time intervals called epochs. At the start of each epoch, the summation of the inputs to each neuron is examined. If it is greater than the threshold, the output becomes one; if it is less than the threshold, it becomes zero. Neuron outputs remain unchanged during an epoch.

The object is to select the resistors (weights) so that a continuously increasing voltage X applied to the single-input terminal produces a set of four outputs representing a binary number, the value of which is an approximation to the input voltage (see Figure 6-5). First, the energy function is defined as follows:

$$E = -1/2[X - \sum_j 2^j\, \mathrm{OUT}_j]^2 + \sum_j (2^{2j-1})[\mathrm{OUT}_j(1 - \mathrm{OUT}_j)] \qquad (6\text{-}7)$$

where X is the input voltage.

When E is minimized, the desired outputs have been reached. The first expression in brackets is minimized when the binary number formed by the outputs is as close as possible (in the least-squares sense) to the analog value of the input X. The second bracketed expression goes to 0 when all of the outputs are either 1 or 0, thereby imposing the constraint that the outputs have only binary values.

If Equation 6-7 is rearranged and compared with Equation 6-2, the resulting expression for the weights is

$$w_{ij} = -2^{(i+j)}$$

$$y_i = 2^i \qquad\qquad (6\text{-}8)$$

where

w_{ij} = conductance (the reciprocal of resistance) from the output

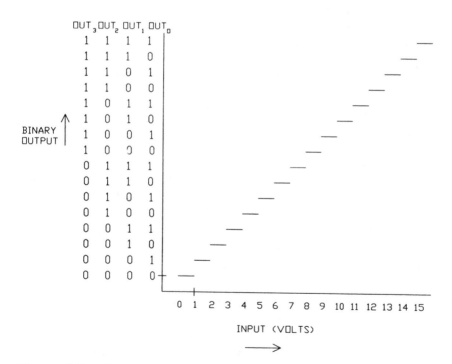

Figure 6-5. Four-Bit Analog-to-Digital Converter Ideal Input–Output Relationship

of neuron i to the input of neuron j (this must also equal the conductance from the output of neuron j to the input of neuron i)

y_i = conductance from the input X to the input of neuron i.

To produce a circuit with practical values of resistance and power dissipation, all weights must be scaled by a multiplicative constant.

The idealized input–output relationship of Figure 6-5 will be realized only if the inputs are set to zero prior to performing a conversion. If this is not done, the network may become trapped in a local minimum of the energy function and produce incorrect outputs.

The Traveling Salesman Problem

The "traveling salesman problem," or TSP, is an optimization task that arises in many practical situations. It may be stated as follows: given a group of cities to be visited and the distance between each city, find the shortest tour that visits each city only once and returns to the starting point. The problem has been proven to be one of a large set of problems termed "NP complete" (nondeterministic polynomial) (Garey and Johnson 1979). NP complete problems have no known method of solution better than trying all the possibilities, nor, according to most mathematicians, is any superior method likely to be found. Because such an exhaustive search is generally impractical for more than a few cities, heuristic methods have been applied to find solutions that are acceptable, if not optimal.

The solution using recurrent networks described by Hopfield and Tank (1985) is typical in that regard; the results are not guaranteed to be optimal. Still, an answer is reached so rapidly that the technique may prove useful in certain cases.

Suppose that the cities to be visited are lettered A, B, C, and D, and that the distance between the pairs is d_{ab}, d_{bc}, and so on.

The solution is an ordered set of n cities. The problem is then to map this onto the computational network, using neurons in the high-gain mode (λ approaching ∞). Each city is represented as a row of n neurons. One and only one such neuron in a row may be set to one (all others must be set to zero). This neuron set to one indicates the order in which a specific city is visited during the tour. Figure 6-6 shows such a result, where city C is visited first, city A is visited second, city D is visited third, and city B is visited fourth. This requires n^2 neurons, a number that grows rapidly with the number of cities. The length of such a tour would be $d_{ca} + d_{ad} + d_{db} + d_{bc}$. Because each city is visited only once, and only one city is visited at a time, there is only a single 1 in each row and column. For an n-city problem there are $n!/(2n)$ distinct tours. If $n = 60$, there are 69.34155×10^{78} possible tours. Considering that there are only 10^{11} stars in the Milky Way galaxy, it becomes clear why calculating all possibilities for a 1,000-city tour would take geological time on the world's fastest computer.

Let us demonstrate how to set up a network to solve such an NP-complete problem. Each neuron is identified by double subscripts, indicating the city and the order in which it is visited. For example, OUT_{xj} indicates that city x was the jth city in the tour.

The energy function must satisfy two requirements: first, it must be low for only those solutions that produce a single 1 in each column and row. Second, it must favor solutions having short paths.

The first requirement is satisfied by the three-summation energy function that follows:

$$E = A/2 \sum_X \sum_i \sum_{j \neq i} OUT_{Xi} \, OUT_{Xj}$$

$$+ B/2 \sum_i \sum_X \sum_{Y \neq X} OUT_{Xi} \, OUT_{Yi}$$

$$+ C/2 \left[\left(\sum_X \sum_i OUT_{Xi} \right) - n \right]^2 \tag{6-9}$$

where A, B, and C are constants. The resulting set of rules is as follows:

1. The first triple summation is zero if, and only if, each row (city) contains no more than a single 1.
2. The second triple summation is zero if, and only if, each column (tour position) contains no more than a single 1.

	ORDER VISITED			
CITY	1	2	3	4
A	0	1	0	0
B	0	0	0	1
C	1	0	0	0
D	0	0	1	0

Figure 6-6.   Traveling Salesman Tour

3. The third summation is zero if, and only if, there are exactly n 1s in the matrix.

The second requirement—favoring short tours—is satisfied by adding a term to the energy function as follows:

$$E = 1/2D\sum_{X}\sum_{Y\neq X}\sum_{i} d_{XY}\,\mathrm{OUT}_{Xi}(\mathrm{OUT}_{Y,i+1} + \mathrm{OUT}_{Y,i-1}) \quad (6\text{-}10)$$

Note that this term represents the length of any valid tour. The subscripts are defined modulo n for convenience; that is, $\mathrm{OUT}_{n+j} = \mathrm{OUT}_j$, where D is a constant.

With sufficiently large values for A, B, and C, the low-energy states will represent valid tours, while a large value for D ensures that a short tour will be found.

Next, the weights must be found. This involves relating the terms in the energy function to those of the general form (see Equation 6-2). The result is as follows:

$w_{xi,yj} = -A\,\delta_{xy}(1 - \delta_{ij})$ (prevents more than a single 1 within a row)

$\quad\quad -B\,\delta_{ij}(1 - \delta_{xy})$ (prevents more than a single 1 in a column)

$\quad\quad -C$ (global inhibition)

$\quad\quad -D\,d_{xy}(\delta_{j,i+1} + \delta_{j,i-1})$ (distance term)

where $\delta_{ij} = 1$ if $i = j$ and otherwise is 0.

In addition, each neuron has a bias weight x_i connected to $+1$ with a value of Cn.

Hopfield and Tank (1985) report an experiment in which the TSP was solved for 10 cities. In this case, they chose the excitation function

$$OUT = 1/2[1 + \tanh (NET/u_0)]$$

As a result, 16 out of 20 trials converged to valid tours, and about 50% of the solutions were one of the shortest tours as found by exhaustive search. This result is more impressive if one realizes that there are 181,440 possible valid tours.

It has been reported that the convergence of Hopfield's solution to the traveling salesman problem is highly dependent upon the coefficients, and that there is no systematic way to determine their values (Van den Bout and Miller 1988). These authors propose another energy function, with only one coefficient the value of which is easily found. In addition, they present a new convergence algorithm. It may be expected that new and better methods will continue to be developed, as a fully satisfactory solution would have many important applications.

DISCUSSION

Local Minima

Starting from suitable initial conditions, the analog-to-digital converter network finds a single optimal solution. This is due to the simple nature of the energy surface for this problem. In the TSP, the energy surface is highly convoluted—full of dips, valleys, and local minima—and there is no guarantee that a global optimal solution will be found, or even that the solution will be valid. This raises serious questions about the reliability of the network and the credibility of its solutions. The limitations of the network are mitigated by the fact that finding global minima for NP-complete problems is an intractable problem that has not been solved in a reasonable amount of time in any other way; methods that are much slower and inherently serial produce results that are no better.

Speed

The rapid computational capability of the network is a major advantage. This arises from the highly parallel nature of the convergence process. If implemented in analog electronics form, solutions seldom take more than a few network time constants. Furthermore, the convergence time changes little with the size of the problem. Contrast this with the more than exponential increase in processing time with conventional approaches. Single-processor simulations cannot take advantage of this inherently parallel architecture, but modern multiprocessor systems, such as the Connection Machine (with 65,536 processors!), hold great promise in solving previously intractable problems.

Energy Function

It is not a trivial matter to find the function that maps a problem onto the general network-energy function. Existing solutions have been achieved through ingenuity and mathematical expertise, talents that are always in short supply. For certain problems, methods exist to determine the network weights in a systematic fashion; these techniques are studied in Chapter 7.

Network Capacity

The maximum number of memories that may be stored in a Hopfield network is a current research topic. Because a network of N binary neurons can have as many as $2N$ states, researchers were surprised to find that the maximum memory storage capacity was much less than this.

If too many memories are stored, the network will not stabilize on some of them. Furthermore, it can remember things it has not been taught; that is, it can stabilize to a solution that is not among the desired vectors. These characteristics perplexed early researchers, who had no mathematical way to determine how many memories could be stored without encountering the problems.

Recent research has cast much light on this matter. For example, it had been conjectured that the maximum number of memories K that can be stored in a network of N neurons and recalled without error is less than cN^2, where c is a positive constant greater than one. While this limit is approached in some cases, in general it proved to be excessively optimistic; Hopfield (1982) showed experimentally that the general capacity limit was actually more like $0.15N$. Abu-Mostafa and St. Jacques (1985) have shown that the number of such states cannot exceed N, a result that is compatible with observations of actual systems and is as good an estimate as is available today.

CONCLUSION

Recurrent networks are fertile subjects for continued research. Their dynamic behavior creates new and interesting possibilities and certain unique problems. As we point out in Chapter 9, the power and problems translate into the optical domain, where they create fascinating image-recognition capability in addition to perplexing limitations.

References

Abu-Mostafa, Y. S., and St. Jacques, J. 1985. Information capacity of the Hopfield model. *IEEE Transactions on Information Theory* 31(4): 461–64.

Cohen, M. A., and Grossberg, S. G. 1983. Absolute stability of global pattern formation and parallel memory storage by competitive neural networks. *IEEE Transactions on Systems, Man and Cybernetics* 13:815–26.

Garey, M. R., and Johnson, D. S. 1979. *Computers and intractability*. New York: W. H. Freeman.

Grossberg, S. 1987. *The adaptive brain*, vols. 1 and 2. Amsterdam: North-Holland.

Hinton, G. E., and Sejnowski, T. J. 1986. Learning and relearning in Boltzmann machines. In *Parallel distributed processing*, vol. 1, pp. 282–317. Cambridge, MA: MIT Press.

Hopfield, J. J. 1982. Neural networks and physical systems with emergent collective computational abilities. *Proceedings of the National Academy of Science* 79:2554–58.

———. 1984. Neurons with graded response have collective computational properties like those of two-state neurons. *Proceedings of the National Academy of Science* 81:3088–92.

Hopfield, J. J., and Tank, D. W. 1985. Neural computation of decisions in optimization problems. *Biological Cybernetics* 52:141–52.

———. 1986. Computing with neural circuits: A model. *Science* 233:625–33.

Tank, D. W., and Hopfield, J. J. 1986. Simple "neural" optimization networks: An A/D converter, signal decision circuit, and a linear programming circuit. *IEEE Transactions on Circuits and Systems* CAS-33(5):533–41.

Van den Bout, D. E., and Miller, T. K. 1988. A traveling salesman objective function that works. *Proceedings of the IEEE International Conference on Neural Networks,* vol. 2, pp. 299–304. San Diego, CA: SOS Printing.

7

Bidirectional Associative Memories

Human memory is often associative; one thing reminds us of another, and that, of still another. If we allow our thoughts to wander, they move from topic to topic based on a chain of mental associations. Alternatively, we can use this associative ability to recover a lost memory. If we have forgotten where we left our glasses, we attempt to remember where we last saw them, who we were speaking to, and what we were doing. We thereby establish one end of an associative link and allow our mind to connect it to the desired memory.

The associative memories discussed in Chapter 6 are, strictly speaking, autoassociative; that is, a memory can be completed or corrected, but cannot be associated with a different memory. This is a result of their single-layer structure, which requires the output vector to appear on the same neurons on which the input vector was applied.

The bidirectional associative memory (BAM) is heteroassociative; that is, it accepts an input vector on one set of neurons and produces a related, but different, output vector on another set. Like the Hopfield net, the BAM is capable of generalization, producing correct outputs despite corrupted inputs. Also, adaptive versions can abstract, extracting the ideal from a set of noisy examples. These characteristics are strongly reminiscent of human mental functions and bring artificial neural networks one step closer to an emulation of the brain.

Recent publications (Kosko 1987a; Kosko and Guest 1987) have presented several forms of bidirectional associative memories. Like most important ideas, this one has deep roots; for example, the work of Grossberg (1982) presents several concepts that are important to BAMs. No attempt is made here to resolve questions of priority among research works; references are provided solely on the basis of their value in illuminating and expanding the subject matter.

BAM STRUCTURE

Figure 7-1 shows the basic BAM configuration. This format is considerably different from that used by Kosko. It was chosen to highlight the similarity to the Hopfield network and to allow extension to systems with more layers. Here an input vector **A** is applied to the weight network **W** and produces a vector of neuron outputs **B**. Vector **B** is then applied to the transpose of the first weight net-

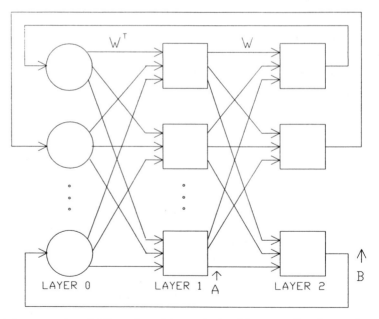

Figure 7-1.   Bidirectional Associative Memory Configuration

work $\mathbf{W}^t$, which produces new outputs for vector $\mathbf{A}$. This process is repeated until the network arrives at a stable point, when neither $\mathbf{A}$ nor $\mathbf{B}$ is changing. Note that the neurons in layers 1 and 2 operate as in other paradigms, producing the sum of the weighted inputs and applying it to the activation function F. This process may be expressed in symbols as follows:

$$b_i = F(\sum_j a_j w_{ij}) \qquad (7\text{-}1)$$

or in vector form

$$\mathbf{B} = F(\mathbf{AW}) \qquad (7\text{-}2)$$

where
    $\mathbf{B}$ = the vector of outputs from layer 2
    $\mathbf{A}$ = the vector of outputs from layer 1
    $\mathbf{W}$ = the weight matrix between layers 1 and 2
    F = the activation function

Similarly,

$$\mathbf{A} = F(\mathbf{BW}^t) \qquad (7\text{-}3)$$

where $\mathbf{W}^t$ is the transpose of matrix $\mathbf{W}$.

As discussed in Chapter 1, Grossberg has shown the advantages of using the familiar sigmoidal (logistic) activation function

$$\text{OUT}_i = 1/(1 + \exp^{-\lambda \, * \, \text{NET}_i}) \qquad (7\text{-}4)$$

where
    OUT_i = the output of neuron i
    NET_i = the weighted sum of the inputs to neuron i
    λ = a constant that determines the slope of the curve

In the simplest version of the BAM, the constant λ is made large, thereby producing an activation function that approaches a simple threshold. For the time being, we shall assume that the threshold function is used.

We shall also assume that there is memory within each neuron in layers 1 and 2, and that their outputs change simultaneously with each "tick" of a master clock, remaining constant between ticks. Therefore, the neurons will obey the rules that follow:

$OUT_i(n + 1) = 1$ if $NET_i(n) > 0$ (OUT$_i$ is 1 if NET$_i$ is positive)
$OUT_i(n + 1) = 0$ if $NET_i(n) < 0$ (OUT$_i$ is 0 if NET$_i$ is negative)
$OUT_i(n + 1) = OUT(n)$ if   (OUT is unchanged if NET = 0)
   $NET(n) = 0$

where $OUT_i(n)$ is the value of an output at time n.

Note that as in networks described previously, layer 0 does no computation and has no memory; it serves only as a distribution point for the outputs of layer 2 to matrix $\mathbf{W}^t$.

RETRIEVING A STORED ASSOCIATION

Long-term memories (or associations) are stored in the weight arrays $\mathbf{W}$ and $\mathbf{W}^t$. Each memory consists of two vectors: $\mathbf{A}$, which appears at the outputs of layer 1, and $\mathbf{B}$, the associated memory that is the output of layer 2. To retrieve an associated memory, all or part of vector $\mathbf{A}$ is momentarily forced onto the outputs of layer 1. $\mathbf{A}$ is then removed and the network is allowed to stabilize, producing the associated vector $\mathbf{B}$ at the output of layer 2. $\mathbf{B}$ then operates through the transpose matrix $\mathbf{W}^t$ to produce a close replica of the original input vector $\mathbf{A}$ at the output of layer 1. Each pass around the loop causes the vector outputs of layers 1 and 2 to come closer to the stored memory, until a stable point is reached and changes cease. This point may be considered to constitute a *resonance*, as the vectors pass back and forth between the layers, always reinforcing the current outputs, but no longer changing them. The state of the neurons represents a short-term memory (STM), as it may be changed quickly by applying another input vector. The values in the weight matrix form a long-term memory (LTM) and are changeable only on a longer time scale, using techniques we discuss later in this chapter.

Kosko (1987a) has shown that the network is acting to minimize a Liapunov energy function in much the same way that a Hopfield network converges (see Chapter 6). Thus, each pass around the loop causes the system to descend toward an energy minimum, the location of which is determined by the values of the weights.

This process may be visualized as a ball bearing rolling on a rubber sheet stretched above a table, with each memory point pressed down to the table's surface. (Figure 7-2 illustrates the analogy with a single memory.) The depressions form a gravitational energy minimum at each memory location, with a surrounding "basin of attraction" sloping downward toward it. The free-rolling ball bearing will enter a basin of attraction and eventually roll downward into the associated energy minimum, where it will remain until removed.

ENCODING THE ASSOCIATIONS

A network is usually trained to recognize a set of memories. These comprise a training set, composed of vector pairs **A** and **B**. This network is trained by calculation; that is, the weight matrix is computed to be the sum of the outer products of all of the vector pairs in the training set. Symbolically,

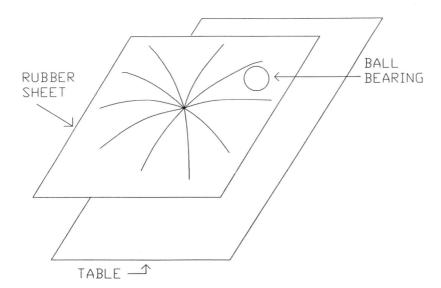

Figure 7-2. Bidirectional Associative Memory Energy Surface

$$\mathbf{W} = \sum_i \mathbf{A}_i'\mathbf{B}_i$$

We assume that the memories consist of binary vectors. This limitation seems less severe if one remembers that the entire contents of the Library of Congress could be encoded into a single, rather lengthy binary vector! Also, Kosko (1987c) has achieved better performance by making the vectors bipolar before performing the outer-product operation. Thus, a vector component greater than zero becomes one, and a component less than or equal to zero becomes minus one.

As an example, let us suppose that we wish to train a network to remember three binary-vector pairs. In this example, the vectors $\mathbf{A}_i$ have the same number of components as the vectors $\mathbf{B}_i$. However, this is not necessary to the algorithm; associations can be formed between vectors of different size.

Original Vector	*Associated Vector*	*Bipolar Versions*	
$\mathbf{A}_1 = (1,0,0)$	$\mathbf{B}_1 = (0,0,1)$	$\mathbf{A}_1' = (1,-1,-1)$	$\mathbf{B}_1' = (-1,-1,1)$
$\mathbf{A}_2 = (0,1,0)$	$\mathbf{B}_2 = (0,1,0)$	$\mathbf{A}_2' = (-1,1,-1)$	$\mathbf{B}_2' = (-1,1,-1)$
$\mathbf{A}_3 = (0,0,1)$	$\mathbf{B}_3 = (1,0,0)$	$\mathbf{A}_3' = (-1,-1,1)$	$\mathbf{B}_3' = (1,-1,-1)$

Computing the weight matrixes

$$\mathbf{W} = \mathbf{A}_1''\mathbf{B}_1' + \mathbf{A}_2''\mathbf{B}_2' + \mathbf{A}_3''\mathbf{B}_3'$$

$$
\begin{array}{ccc}
-1 & -1 & 1 \\
1 & 1 & -1 \\
1 & 1 & -1
\end{array}
+
\begin{array}{ccc}
1 & -1 & 1 \\
-1 & 1 & -1 \\
1 & -1 & 1
\end{array}
+
\begin{array}{ccc}
-1 & 1 & 1 \\
-1 & -1 & 1 \\
1 & -1 & -1
\end{array}
=
\begin{array}{ccc}
-1 & -1 & 3 \\
-1 & 3 & -1 \\
3 & -1 & -1
\end{array}
$$

Now, applying an input vector $\mathbf{A}_1 = (1,0,0)$, we compute the output vector $\mathbf{O}$

$$
\mathbf{O} = \mathbf{A}_1'\mathbf{W} = (1\ 0\ 0)
\begin{array}{ccc}
-1 & -1 & 3 \\
-1 & 3 & -1 \\
3 & -1 & -1
\end{array}
=
\begin{array}{ccc}
-1 & -1 & 3
\end{array}
$$

Next, applying the threshold rule:

$b_i = 1$ if $o_i > 0$
$b_i = 0$ if $o_i < 0$
b_i unchanged if $o_i = 0$

$$\mathbf{B_1}' = (0\ 0\ 1)$$

which is the desired association. Then, applying $\mathbf{B_1}'$ around the loop to $\mathbf{W}^t$

$$\mathbf{B_1}'\mathbf{W}^t = (0\ 0\ 1) \begin{array}{ccc} -1 & -1 & 3 \\ -1 & 3 & -1 \\ 3 & -1 & -1 \end{array} = (3\ -1\ -1)$$

which becomes $(1, 0, 0)$ after thresholding, returning the value of $\mathbf{A_1}$.

This example shows that applying an input vector to $\mathbf{A}$ through $\mathbf{W}$ produces its associated output vector at $\mathbf{B}$. This in turn is applied through $\mathbf{W}^t$ to again produce $\mathbf{A}$. In this way, a resonance is formed around the loop.

The BAM has the capability to generalize. For example, if an incomplete or partially incorrect vector is applied at $\mathbf{A}$, the network tends to produce the closest memory at $\mathbf{B}$, which in turn tends to correct the errors in $\mathbf{A}$. Several passes may be required, but the network converges to the nearest stored memory.

Feedback systems can be prone to oscillations; that is, they can wander from state to state and never stabilize. Kosko (1987a) has proven, however, that all BAMs are unconditionally stable for any weight network. This important characteristic arises from the transpose relationship between the two weight networks, and means that any set of associations may be learned without risk of instability.

There is a close relationship between the BAM and the Hopfield networks described in Chapter 6. If the weight matrix $\mathbf{W}$ is made square and symmetrical, then $\mathbf{W} = \mathbf{W}^t$. In this case, if layers 1 and 2 are the same set of neurons, the BAM reduces to the autoassociative Hopfield net.

MEMORY CAPACITY

Like the Hopfield network, the BAM has restrictions on the maximum number of associations it can accurately recall. If this limit is exceeded, the network may produce incorrect outputs, remembering associations that it has not been taught.

Kosko (1987a) has estimated that in general the maximum number of stored associations cannot exceed the number of neurons in the smaller layer. This assumes that the capacity has been maximized through "even coding," that is, when the number of plus-one components equals the number of minus-one components in each bipolar vector. This estimate has turned out to be somewhat optimistic. The work of McEliece, Posner, Rodemich, and Venkatesh (1987) on the capacity of the Hopfield network can be easily extended to the BAM. It shows that if L is randomly chosen and even coded, and if stable vectors are applied to a BAM, and if L is less than $n/(2 \log_2 n)$, where n is the number of neurons in the smaller layer, then all but a "small fraction" of the stored memories can be retrieved. For example, if $n = 1,024$, then L must be less than 51. If all memories must be recalled, L must be less than $n/(4 \log_2 n)$, which is 25. These rather discouraging results imply that large systems can store only modest numbers of associations.

Recent work by Haines and Hecht-Nielsen (1988) has shown that the BAM can have up to 2^n stable states, if a threshold term T is selected for each neuron. This configuration, which they have termed a nonhomogeneous BAM, is an extension of the original homogeneous BAM, in which the thresholds are all zero. The modified neuron-transfer function becomes

$\text{OUT}_i(n + 1) = 1$ if $\text{NET}_i(n) > T_i$ (OUT$_i$ is 1 if NET$_i$ is greater than the threshold)

$\text{OUT}_i(n + 1) = 0$ if $\text{NET}_i(n) < T_i$ (OUT$_i$ is 0 if NET$_i$ is less than the threshold)

$\text{OUT}_i(n + 1) = \text{OUT}_i(n)$ if $\text{NET}_i(n) = T_i$ (OUT$_i$ unchanged if NET$_i$ equals the threshold)

where $\text{OUT}_i(t)$ is the output of neuron i at time t.

By choosing an appropriate threshold for each neuron, the number of stable states can be made anything from 1 to 2^n, where n is the number of neurons in the smaller layer. Unfortunately, these states cannot be selected randomly; they are determined by a rigid geometrical procedure. If the user selects L states at random, where L is less than $(0.68)n^2/\{[\log_2 (n)] + 4\}^2$, and if each vector has $4 + \log_2 n$ entries equal to $+1$ and the rest equal to -1, then it is possible to construct a nonhomogeneous BAM with 98% of these vectors as stable states. For example, if $n = 1,024$, then L must be less than 3,637, a major improvement over the homogeneous BAM, but far less than the 2^{1024} states that are possible.

The restriction on the number of ones in the input vectors constitutes a serious problem. As yet, we have no theory that enables us to code an arbitrary set of vectors into such a "sparse set." Perhaps more serious is the problem of incorrect convergence; that is, the network may not produce the closest association. This is due to the nature of the basins of attraction; little is known about their shape. This means that the BAM is not a nearest-neighbor associator. In fact, it may produce associations that are only slightly related to the input vector. As with the homogeneous BAM, spurious stable states can occur and little is understood about their number or nature.

Despite these problems, the BAM remains the subject of intensive research. It has the virtue of simplicity. In addition, it can be implemented in large-scale integrated circuits (either analog or digital), making it potentially inexpensive. As our knowledge increases, the BAM's limitations may be removed. In that case, it could prove, in both experimental and practical application, to be a highly useful artificial neural network.

CONTINUOUS BAM

In the preceding discussion, the neurons in layers 1 and 2 are considered to be synchronous; that is, each neuron contains memory, so that all neurons change state simultaneously upon the occurrence of a pulse from a central clock. In an asynchronous system, any neuron is free to change state at any time that its input indicates that it should do so.

Also, a simple threshold has been used as the neuron's activation function, thereby producing a discontinuity in the neuron's transfer function. Both synchronous operation and discontinuous functions are biologically implausible and quite unnecessary; continuous, asynchronous BAMs discard both of these stipulations and function in much the same way as the discrete versions. It might seem that such systems would suffer from instability. Fortunately, Kosko (1987a) has shown that every continuous BAM is stable (but still subject to the capacity limits discussed above).

Grossberg (1973, 1976, 1978, 1980) has shown the sigmoid to be the optimal activation function due to its ability to enhance low-level signals while compressing the neuron's dynamic range. The continuous BAM can use the sigmoid function with values of λ near one, thereby producing neurons that respond smoothly and continuously, much like their biological prototypes.

The continuous BAM lends itself to analog implementations constructed of resistors and amplifiers. Very large-scale integration (VLSI) realizations of such networks appear feasible and economically attractive. The optical versions that are covered in Chapter 9 are even more promising.

THE ADAPTIVE BAM

In versions of the BAM considered so far, the weight matrix is calculated as the sum of the outer products of the input-vector pairs. This calculation is useful in that it demonstrates the functions that a BAM can represent. However, it is certainly not the way that weights are determined in the brain.

The adaptive BAM adjusts its weights during operation; that is, application of the training-vector set causes it to dig its own energy wells in which to resonate. Gradually, short-term memory seeps into long-term memory, modifying the network as a function of its experience. The network is trained by applying vectors to layer A and associated vectors to layer B. Either one or both vectors may be noisy versions of the ideal; within limits, the network learns the idealized vectors free of noise. In this sense, it abstracts the essence of the associations, learning ideals when it has seen only noisy approximations.

Because the continuous BAM has been proven stable regardless of the weights, slow changes in the weights would not be expected to upset this stability. Kosko (1987b) has shown this to be the case.

The simplest training algorithm uses Hebbian learning (Hebb 1949), where the change in a weight is proportional to the product of the activation level of its source neuron and that of its destination neuron. Symbolically

$$\delta\, w_{ij} = \eta * (\text{OUT}_i\text{OUT}_j) \tag{7-5}$$

where

   $\delta\, w_{ij}$ = the change in a specific weight connecting neuron i to neuron j in either matrix **W** or **W**^{t}
   OUT$_i$ = the output of neuron i in layer 1 or 2
   η = a positive learning rate coefficient less than 1

THE COMPETITIVE BAM

In many biological neural systems, some sort of competition is observed between neurons. In the neurons that process signals from the retina, lateral inhibition tends to increase the output of the most highly activated neuron at the expense of its neighbors. This rich-get-richer system increases contrast by raising the activation level of the neurons connected to bright areas of the retina, while further reducing the outputs of those "viewing" darker areas.

In the BAM, competition is implemented by interconnecting neurons within each layer by means of additional weights. These form another weight matrix, with positive weights on the main diagonal and negative weights at other positions. The Cohen-Grossberg theorem (Cohen and Grossberg 1983) shows that such a network is unconditionally stable if the weight arrays are symmetrical. As a practical matter, the networks are usually stable even without symmetry. However, it is not known which classes of weight patterns can lead to unstable operation.

DISCUSSION

The BAM's limited storage capacity, spurious responses, and somewhat unpredictable behavior has led some to regard it as obsolete.

This conclusion is certainly premature. The BAM has many advantages: it is compatible with analog circuits and optical systems; it converges rapidly in both the learning and retrieval phases; and it offers simplicity and an intuitively appealing mode of operation. Theory is developing at a rapid rate, and methods may be found that explain the BAM's idiosyncrasies and overcome its problems.

References

Cohen, M., and Grossberg, S. 1983. Absolute stability of global pattern formation and parallel memory storage by competitive neural networks. *IEEE Transactions on Systems, Man, and Cybernetics* SMC-13:815–926.

Grossberg, S. 1973. Contour enhancement, short term memory, and constancies in reverberating neural networks. *Studies in Applied Mathematics* 52:217–57.

_____. 1976. Adaptive pattern classification and universal recoding, I: Parallel development and coding of neural feature detectors. *Biological Cybernetics* 23:187–202.

_____. 1978. A theory of human memory: Self-organization and performance of sensory-motor codes, maps, and plans. In *Progress in theoretical biology*, vol. 5, ed. R. Rosen and F. Snell. New York: Academic Press.

_____. 1980. How does the brain build a cognitive code? *Psychological Review* 1:1–51.

_____. 1982. *Studies of mind and brain.* Boston: Reidel Press.

Haines, K., and Hecht-Nielsen, R. 1988. A BAM with increased information storage capacity. *Proceedings of the IEEE International Conference on Neural Networks*, vol 1, pp. 181–190. San Diego, CA: SOS Printing.

Hebb, D. O. 1949. *The organization of behavior.* New York: Wiley.

Kosko, B. (1987a). Bi-directional associative memories. *IEEE Transactions on Systems, Man and Cybernetics* 18(1):49–60.

_____. 1987b. Competitive adaptive bi-directional associative memories. In *Proceedings of the IEEE First International Conference on Neural Networks*, eds. M. Caudill and C. Butler, vol. 2, pp. 759–66. San Diego, CA: SOS Printing.

_____. 1987c. Constructing an associative memory. *Byte*, September, pp. 137–44.

Kosko, B., and Guest, C. 1987. Optical bi-directional associative memories. *Society for Photo-optical and Instrumentation Engineers Proceedings: Image Understanding* 758:11–18.

McEliece, R. J., Posner, E. C., Rodemich, E. R., and Venkatesh, S. S. 1987. The capacity of the Hopfield associative memory. *IEEE Transactions on Information Theory* IT-33:461–82.

8

Adaptive Resonance Theory

The human brain performs the formidable task of sorting a continuous flood of sensory information received from the environment. From a deluge of trivia, it must extract vital information, act upon it, and perhaps file it away in long-term memory. Understanding human memorization presents serious problems; new memories are stored in such a fashion that existing ones are not forgotten or modified. This creates a dilemma: how can the brain remain plastic, able to record new memories as they arrive, and yet retain the stability needed to ensure that existing memories are not erased or corrupted in the process?

Conventional artificial neural networks have failed to solve the stability–plasticity dilemma. Too often, learning a new pattern erases or modifies previous training. In some cases, this is unimportant. If there is only a fixed set of training vectors, the network can be cycled through these repeatedly and may eventually learn them all. In a backpropagation network, for example, the training vectors are applied sequentially until the network has learned the entire set. If, however, a fully trained network must learn a new training vector, it may disrupt the weights so badly that complete retraining is required.

In a real-world case, the network will be exposed to a constantly changing environment; it may never see the same training vector twice. Under such circumstances, a backpropagation network will often learn nothing; it will continuously modify its weights to no avail, never arriving at satisfactory settings.

Even worse, Carpenter and Grossberg (1986) have shown examples of a network in which only four training patterns, presented cyclically, will cause network weights to change continuously, never converging. This temporal instability is one of the main factors that led Grossberg and his associates to explore radically different configurations. Adaptive resonance theory, or ART, is one result of research into this problem (Carpenter and Grossberg 1987a; Grossberg 1987).

ART networks and algorithms maintain the plasticity required to learn new patterns, while preventing the modification of patterns that have been learned previously. This capability has stimulated a great deal of interest, but many people have found the theory difficult to understand. The mathematics behind ART are complicated, but the fundamental ideas and implementations are not. We concentrate here on the actual operation of ART; those who are more mathematically inclined will find an abundance of theory in the references. Our objective is to provide enough concrete information in algorithmic form so that the reader can understand the basic ideas and, perhaps, write computer simulations to explore the characteristics of this important network.

ART ARCHITECTURE

Adaptive resonance theory is divided into two paradigms, each defined by the form of the input data and its processing. ART-1 is designed to accept only binary input vectors, whereas ART-2, a later development that generalizes ART-1, can classify both binary and continuous inputs. Only ART-1 is presented in this volume. The reader interested in ART-2 is referred to Carpenter and Grossberg (1987b) for a complete treatment of this significant development. For brevity, ART-1 is referred to as ART in the paragraphs that follow.

An Overview of ART

The ART network is a vector classifier. It accepts an input vector and classifies it into one of a number of categories depending upon which of a number of stored patterns it most resembles. Its classification decision is indicated by the single recognition layer that fires (see Figure 8-1). If the input vector does not match any stored pattern, a new category is created by storing a pattern that is like the input vector. Once a stored pattern is found that matches the input vector within a specified tolerance (the vigilance), that pattern is adjusted (trained) to make it still more like the input vector.

No stored pattern is ever modified if it does not match the current input pattern within the vigilance tolerance. In this way, the stability–plasticity dilemma is resolved; new patterns from the environment can create additional classification categories, but a new input pattern cannot cause an existing memory to be changed unless the two match closely.

A Simplified ART Architecture

Figure 8-1 shows a simplified ART network configuration drawn as five functional modules. It consists of two layers of neurons labeled "comparison" and "recognition." Gain 1, Gain 2, and Reset provide control functions needed for training and classification.

Before proceeding to the network's overall function, it is neces-

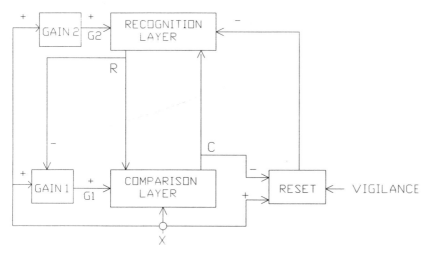

Figure 8-1. Simplified Adaptive Resonance Theory Network

sary to understand the internal operation of the modules; the discussion that follows describes each of them.

Comparison Layer

The comparison layer receives the binary input vector **X** and initially passes it through unchanged to become the vector **C**. In a later phase, binary vector **R** is produced from the recognition layer, modifying **C** as described below.

Each neuron in the comparison layer (see Figure 8-2) receives three binary inputs (zero or one): (1) a component x_i from the input vector **X**; (2) the feedback signal P_j, the weighted sum of the recognition layer outputs; and (3) an input from the gain signal Gain 1 (the same signal goes to all neurons in this layer).

To output a one, at least two of a neuron's three inputs must be one; otherwise, its output is zero. This implements the "two-thirds rule," described by Carpenter and Grossberg (1987b). Ini-

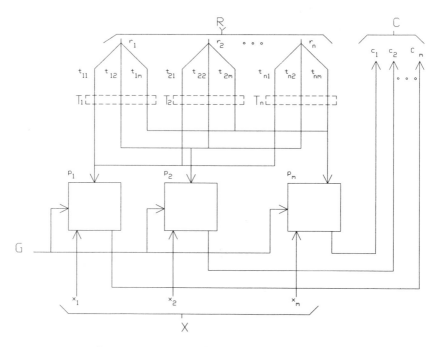

Figure 8-2. Simplified Comparison Layer

tially, gain signal Gain 1 is set to one, providing one of the needed inputs, and all components of the vector **R** are set to zero; hence, vector **C** starts out identical to the binary input vector **X**.

Recognition Layer

The recognition layer serves to classify the input vector. Each recognition layer neuron has an associated weight vector $\mathbf{B}_j$. Only the neuron with a weight vector best matching the input vector "fires"; all others are inhibited.

As illustrated in Figure 8-3, a neuron in the recognition layer responds maximally when the vector **C** from the comparison layer matches its set of weights; hence, these weights constitute a stored pattern or exemplar, an idealized example, for a category of input vectors. These weights are real numbers, not binary valued. A binary version of the same pattern is also stored in a corresponding set of weights in the comparison layer (see Figure 8-2); this set con-

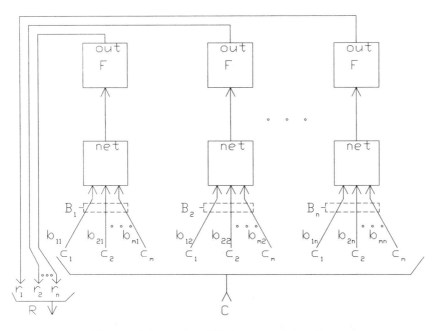

Figure 8-3. Simplified Recognition Layer

sists of those weights that connect to a specific recognition-layer neuron, one weight per comparison-layer neuron.

In operation, each recognition-layer neuron computes a dot product between its weights and the incoming vector **C**. The neuron that has weights most like the vector **C** will have the largest output, thereby winning the competition while inhibiting all other neurons in the layer.

As shown in Figure 8-4, the neurons in the recognition layer are interconnected by a lateral-inhibition network. In the simplest case (the only one considered in this volume), this ensures that only one neuron "fires" at a time (i.e., only the neuron with the highest activation level will output a one; all others will be zero). This competitive, winner-take-all response is achieved by connecting a negative weight l_{ij} from each neuron's output r_i to the input of the other neurons. Thus, if a neuron has a large output it inhibits all other neurons in the layer. Also, each neuron has a positive weight from its output to its own input. If a neuron's output is at a one level, this feedback tends to reinforce and sustain it.

Gain 2

G2, the output of Gain 2, is one if input vector **X** has any component that is one. More precisely, G2 is the logical "or" of the components of **X**.

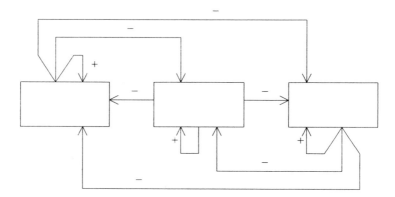

Figure 8-4.   Lateral Inhibition-Recognition Layer

Gain 1

Like G2, the output of Gain 1 is one if any component of the binary input vector **X** is one; however, if any component of **R** is one, G1 is forced to zero. The table that follows shows this relationship:

"Or" of **X** Components	"Or" of **R** Components	G2
0	0	0
1	0	1
1	1	0
0	1	0

Reset

The reset module measures the similarity between vectors **X** and **C**. If they differ by more than the vigilance parameter, a reset signal is sent to disable the firing neuron in the recognition layer.

In operation, the reset module calculates similarity as the ratio of the number of ones in the vector **C** to the number of ones in the vector **X**. If this ratio is below the vigilance parameter level, the reset signal is issued.

ART Classification Operation

The ART classification process consists of three major phases: recognition, comparison, and search.

The Recognition Phase

Initially, no input vector is applied; hence, all components of input vector **X** are zero. This sets G2 to zero, thereby disabling all recognition-layer neurons and causing their outputs to be zero. Because all recognition-layer neurons start out in the same state, all have an equal chance to win the subsequent competition.

The vector to be classified, **X**, is now applied. It must have one or more components that are one, thereby making both G1 and G2 equal to one. This "primes" all of the comparison-layer neurons, providing one of the two inputs required by the two-thirds rule, thereby allowing a neuron to fire if the corresponding component of the **X** input vector is one. Thus, during this phase, vector **C** is an exact duplicate of **X**.

Next, for each neuron in the recognition layer a dot product is formed between its associated weight vector B_j and the vector **C** (see Figure 8-4). The neuron with the largest dot product has weights that best match the input vector. It wins the competition and fires, inhibiting all other outputs from this layer. This makes a single component r_j of vector **R** (see Figure 8-1) equal to one, and all other components equal to zero.

To summarize, the ART network stores a set of patterns in the weights associated with the recognition-layer neurons, one for each classification category. The recognition-layer neuron with weights that best match the applied vector fires, its output be-comes one, and all other outputs from this layer are forced to zero.

The Comparison Phase

The single neuron firing in the recognition layer passes a one back to the comparison layer on its output signal r_j. This single one may be visualized as fanning out, going through a separate binary weight t_{ji} to each neuron in the comparison layer, providing each with a signal p_i, which is equal to the value of t_{ji} (one or zero) (see Figure 8-5).

The initialization and training algorithms ensure that each weight vector T_j consists of binary valued weights; also, each weight vector B_j constitutes a scaled version of the corresponding weight vector T_j. This means that all components of **P**, the comparison-layer exci-tation vector, are also binary valued.

Since the vector **R** is no longer all zeros, Gain 1 is inhibited and its output set to zero. Thus, in accordance with the two-thirds rule, the only comparison-layer neurons that will fire are those that receive simultaneous ones from the input vector **X** and the vector **P**.

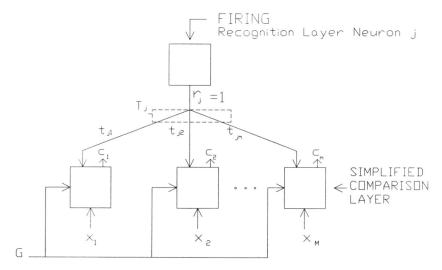

Figure 8-5.   Signal Path for a Single-Firing Recognition-Layer Neuron

In other words, the top-down feedback from the recognition layer acts to force components of **C** to zero in cases in which the input does not match the stored pattern, that is, when **X** and **P** do not have coincident ones.

If there is a substantial mismatch between the **X** and **P** (few coincident ones), few neurons in the comparison layer will fire and **C** will contain many zeros, while **X** contains ones. This indicates that the pattern **P** being fed back is not the one sought and the neuron firing in the recognition layer should be inhibited. This inhibition is performed by the reset block in Figure 8-1, which compares the input vector **X** to the **C** vector and causes the reset signal to occur if their degree of similarity is less than the vigilance level. The effect of the reset is to force the output of the firing neuron in the recognition layer to zero, disabling it for the duration of the current classification.

The Search Phase

If there is no reset signal generated, the match is adequate and the classification is finished. Otherwise, other stored patterns must be searched to seek a better match. In the latter case, the inhibition of the firing neuron in the recognition layer causes all components of the vector **R** to return to zero, G1 goes to one, and input pattern **X** once again appears at **C**. As a result, a different neuron wins in the recognition layer and a different stored pattern **P** is fed back to the comparison layer. If **P** does not match **X**, that firing recognition-layer neuron is also inhibited. This process repeats, neuron by neuron, until one of two events occurs:

1. A stored pattern is found that matches **X** above the level of the vigilance parameter, that is, $S > \rho$. If this occurs, the network enters a training cycle that modifies the weights in both $\mathbf{T}_j$ and $\mathbf{B}_j$, the weight vectors associated with the firing recognition layer neuron.
2. All stored patterns have been tried, found to mismatch the input vector, and all recognition-layer neurons are inhibited. If this is the case, a previously unallocated neuron in the recognition layer is assigned to this pattern and its weight vectors $\mathbf{B}_j$ and $\mathbf{T}_j$ are set to match the input pattern.

Performance Issues

The network described must perform a sequential search through all of its stored patterns. In an analog implementation, this will occur very rapidly; however, it can be a time-consuming process in a simulation on a conventional serial digital computer. If, however, the ART network is implemented with parallel processors, all dot products in the recognition layer can be performed simultaneously. In this case, the search will be very rapid.

The stabilization time required for the lateral-inhibition network can also be lengthy in a serial digital computer. For lateral inhibition to select a "winner," all neurons in the layer are involved in simultaneous computation and communication. This can require a substantial amount of computation before convergence occurs. A feedforward lateral-inhibition network as used in the neocognitron can substantially reduce this time (see Chapter 10).

ART IMPLEMENTATION

Overview

ART, as it is generally found in the literature, is something more than a philosophy, but much less concrete than a computer program. This has allowed a wide range of implementations that adhere to the spirit of ART, while they differ greatly in detail. The implementation that follows is based on Lippman (1987), with certain aspects changed for compatibility with Carpenter and Grossberg (1987a) and the conventions of this volume. This treatment is typical, but other successful implementations differ greatly.

ART Operation

Considered in more detail, the operation of an ART system consists of five phases: initialization, recognition, comparison, search, and training.

Initialization

Before starting the network training process, all weight vectors $\mathbf{B}_j$ and $\mathbf{T}_j$ as well as the vigilance parameter ρ must be set to initial values.

The weights of the bottom-up vectors $\mathbf{B}_j$ are all initialized to the same low value. According to Carpenter and Grossberg (1987a), this should be

$$b_{ij} < L/(L - 1 + m) \quad \text{for all } i, j \tag{8-1}$$

where
    m = the number of components in the input vector
    L = a constant > 1 (typically, $L = 2$)

This value is critical; if it is too large the network can allocate all recognition-layer neurons to a single input vector.

The weights of the top-down vectors $\mathbf{T}_j$ are all initialized to 1, so

$$t_{ji} = 1 \quad \text{for all } j, i \tag{8-2}$$

This value is also critical; Carpenter and Grossberg (1987a) prove that top-down weights that are too small will result in no matches at the comparison layer and no training.

The vigilance parameter ρ is set in the range from 0 to 1, depending upon the degree of mismatch that is to be accepted between the stored pattern and the input vector. At a high value of ρ, the network makes fine distinctions. On the other hand, a low value causes the grouping of input patterns that may be only slightly similar. It may be desirable to change the vigilance during the training process, making only coarse distinctions at the start, and then gradually increasing the vigilance to produce accurate categorization at the end.

Recognition

Application of an input vector **X** initiates the recognition phase. Because initially there is no output from the recognition layer, G1 is set to 1 by the "or" of **X**, providing all comparison-layer neurons with one of the two inputs needed for it to fire (as required by the two-thirds rule). As a result, any component of **X** that is one provides the second input, thereby causing its associated comparison-layer neuron to fire and output a one. Thus, at this time, the vector **C** will be identical to **X**.

As discussed previously, recognition is performed as a dot product for each neuron in the recognition layer, and is expressed as follows:

$$\text{NET}_j = (\mathbf{B}_j \cdot \mathbf{C}) \tag{8-3}$$

where

$\mathbf{B}_j$ = the weight vector associated with recognition-layer neuron j

$\mathbf{C}$ = the output vector of the comparison-layer neuron; at this time, **C** is equal to **X**

NET_j = the excitation of neuron j in the recognition layer

F is the threshold function that follows:

$$OUT_j = 1 \text{ if } NET_j > T \qquad (8\text{-}4)$$
$$0 \text{ otherwise}$$

where T is a threshold.

Lateral inhibition is assumed to exist but is ignored here to simplify these equations. It ensures that only the recognition-layer neuron with the highest value for NET will have an output of one; all others will output zero. It is quite possible to devise systems in which more than one recognition-layer neuron fires at a time, but this is beyond the scope of this volume.

Comparison

At this point, the feedback signal from the recognition layer causes G1 to go to zero; the two-thirds rule permits only those comparison-layer neurons to fire that have corresponding components of the vectors **P** and **X** both equal to one.

The reset block compares the vector **C** to the input vector **X**, producing a reset output whenever their similarity S is below the vigilance threshold. Computing this similarity is simplified by the fact that both vectors are binary (all elements are either one or zero). The procedure that follows computes the required measure of similarity.

1. Call D the number of 1s in the **X** vector.
2. Call N the number of 1s in the **C** vector.

Then compute the similarity S as follows:

$$S = N/D \qquad (8\text{-}5)$$

For example, suppose that

$$\mathbf{X} = 1\ 0\ 1\ 1\ 1\ 0\ 1 \quad \text{then } D = 5$$
$$\mathbf{C} = 0\ 0\ 1\ 1\ 1\ 0\ 1 \quad \text{then } N = 4$$
$$S = N/D = 0.8$$

S will vary from 1 (perfect match) to 0 (worst mismatch).

Note that the two-thirds rule makes **C** the logical "and" of the input vector **X** with the vector **P**. But **P** is equal to $\mathbf{T}_j$, the weight vector from the winning neuron. Thus, D may be found as the number of 1s in the logical "and" of $\mathbf{T}_j$ with **X**.

Search

If the similarity S of the winning neuron is greater than the vigilance, no search is required. If, however, the network has been previously trained, application of an input vector that is not identical to any seen before may fire a recognition-layer neuron with a match below the vigilance level. Due to the training algorithm, it is possible that a different recognition-layer neuron will provide a better match, exceeding the vigilance level, even though the dot product between its weight vector and the input vector may be lower. An example of this situation is shown below.

If the similarity is below the vigilance level, the stored patterns must be searched, seeking one that matches the input vector more closely, or failing that, terminating on an uncommitted neuron that will then be trained. To initiate the search, the reset signal temporarily disables the firing neuron in the recognition layer for the duration of the search, G1 goes to one, and a different recognition-layer neuron wins the competition. Its pattern is then tested for similarity and the process repeats until either a recognition-layer neuron wins the competition with similarity greater than the vigilance (a successful search), or all committed recognition-layer neurons have been tried and disabled (unsuccessful search).

An unsuccessful search will automatically terminate on an uncommitted neuron, as its top-down weights are all ones, their initial values. Thus, the two-thirds rule will make the vector **C** identical to **X**, the similarity S will be one, and the vigilance will be satisfied.

Training

Training is the process in which a set of input vectors are presented sequentially to the input of the network, and the network weights are so adjusted that similar vectors activate the same recognition-layer neuron. Note that this is unsupervised training; there is no teacher and no target vector to indicate the desired response.

Carpenter and Grossberg (1987a) distinguish two kinds of training: slow and fast. In slow training, an input vector may be applied so briefly that network weights do not have enough time to reach their asymptotic values during a single presentation. Thus, the weights will be determined by the statistics of the input vectors rather than by the characteristics of any one. The differential equations of slow training describe the network dynamics during the training process.

Fast training is a special case of slow training that applies if the input vectors are applied for a long enough period of time to allow the weights to approach their final values. In this case, the training formulas involve only algebraic equations. Also, top-down weights assume only binary values rather than the continuous range required in fast training. Only fast training is described in this volume; the interested reader can find an excellent treatment of the more general, slow-training case in Carpenter and Grossberg (1987a).

The training algorithm that follows is applied in both successful and unsuccessful searches.

Set the vector of bottom-up weights $\mathbf{B}_j$ (associated with the firing recognition-layer neuron j) to the normalized values of the vector $\mathbf{C}$. Carpenter and Grossberg (1987a) calculate these weights as follows:

$$b_{ij} = (L\ c_i)/\left(L - 1 + \sum_k c_k\right) \qquad (8\text{-}6)$$

where

$\quad c_i$ = the ith component of the comparison-layer output vector
$\quad j$ = the number of the winning recognition-layer neuron
$\quad b_{ij}$ = the bottom-up weight in $\mathbf{B}_j$ connecting neuron i in the comparison layer to neuron j in the recognition layer
$\quad L$ = a constant > 1 (typically 2)

Weights in the vector $\mathbf{T}_j$ that are associated with the new stored pattern are adjusted so that they equal the corresponding binary values in the vector $\mathbf{C}$:

$$t_{ji} = c_i \quad \text{for all } i \qquad (8\text{-}7)$$

where t_{ji} is the weight from the winning neuron j in the recognition layer neuron i in the comparison layer.

AN ART TRAINING EXAMPLE

In outline, the network is trained by adjusting the top-down and bottom-up weights so that the application of an input pattern causes the network to activate the recognition-layer neuron associated with a similar stored pattern. Furthermore, training is accomplished in a fashion that does not destroy patterns that were learned previously, thereby preventing temporal instability. This task is controlled by the level of the vigilance parameter. A novel input pattern (one that the network has not seen before) will fail to match stored patterns within the tolerance imposed by the vigilance level, thereby causing a new stored pattern to be formed. An input pattern sufficiently like a stored pattern will not form a new exemplar; it will simply modify one that it resembles. Thus, with a suitable setting of the vigilance level, new input patterns already learned and temporal instability are avoided.

Figure 8-6 shows a typical ART training session. Letters are shown as patterns of small squares on an 8-by-8 grid. Each square

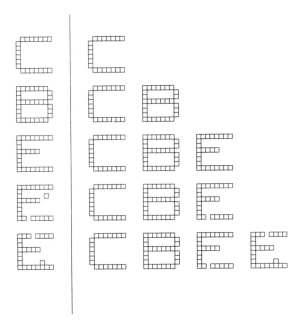

Figure 8-6. ART Training Session

on the left represents a component of the **X** vector with a value of one; all squares not shown are components with values of zero. Letters on the right represent the stored patterns; each is the set of the values of the components of a vector $\mathbf{T}_j$.

First, the letter C is input to the newly initialized system. Because there is no stored pattern that matches it within the vigilance limit, the search phase fails; a new neuron is assigned in the recognition layer, and the weights $\mathbf{T}_j$ are set to equal the corresponding components of the input vector, with weights $\mathbf{B}_j$ becoming a scaled version.

Next, the letter B is presented. This also fails in the search phase and another new neuron is assigned. This is repeated for the letter E. Then, a slightly corrupted version of the letter E is presented to the network. It is close enough to the stored E to pass the vigilance test, so it is used to train the network. The missing pixel in the lower leg of the E produces a zero in the corresponding position of the vector **C**, causing the training algorithm to set that weight of the stored pattern to zero, thereby reproducing the break in the stored pattern. The extra isolated square does not corrupt the stored pattern, as there is no corresponding one introduced into it.

The fourth character is an E, with two different errors. This fails to match a stored pattern (S is less than the ρ), so the search fails and a new neuron is assigned.

This example illustrates the importance of setting the vigilance parameter correctly. If the vigilance is too high, most patterns will fail to match those in storage and the network will create a new neuron for each of them. This results in poor generalization, as minor variations of the same pattern become separate categories. These categories proliferate, all available recognition-layer neurons are assigned, and the system's ability to incorporate new data halts. Conversely, if the vigilance is too low, totally different letters will be grouped together, distorting the stored pattern until it bears little resemblance to any of them.

Unfortunately, there is no theory to guide the setting of the vigilance parameter; one must first decide what degree of difference between patterns will constitute a different category. The boundaries between categories are often "fuzzy" and *a priori* decisions on a large set of input examples may be prohibitively difficult.

Carpenter and Grossberg (1987a) propose a feedback process to adjust the vigilance, whereby incorrect categorization results in "punishment" from an outside agency that acts to raise the vigilance. Such a system requires a standard to determine if the classification was incorrect.

CHARACTERISTICS OF ART

The ART system has a number of important characteristics that are not obvious. The formulas and algorithms may seem arbitrary, whereas in fact, they have been carefully chosen to satisfy theorems regarding system performance. This section discusses some of the implications of the ART algorithms, thereby showing the reasoning behind the design of the initialization and training formulas.

Top-Down Weight Initialization

From the earlier training example it may be seen that the two-thirds rule makes vector C the "and" between the input vector X, and the winning stored vector T_j. That is, only if corresponding components of each are one will that component of C be one. After training, these components of T_j remain one; all others are forced to zero.

This explains why the top-down weights must be initialized to ones. If they were initialized to zeros, all components of vector C would be zero regardless of the input vector components, and the training algorithm would prevent the weights from being anything but zero.

Training may be viewed as a process of "pruning" components of the stored vectors that do not match the input vectors. This process is irreversible; that is, once a top-down weight has been set to zero, the training algorithm can never restore it to a one.

This characteristic has important implications for the learning process. Suppose that a group of closely related vectors should be classified into the same category, indicated by their firing the same recognition-layer neuron. If they are presented sequentially to the network, the first will be assigned a recognition-layer neuron; its weights will be trained to match the input vector. Training with the rest of the vectors will set the weights of the stored vector to zero in all positions where they coincide with zeros from any of these input vectors. Thus, the stored vector comes to represent the logical intersection of all of the training vectors and may be thought of as encoding the essential features of a category of input vectors. A new vector consisting only of these essential features will be assigned to this category; thus, the network correctly recognizes a pattern it has never seen before, an ability reminiscent of human abstraction.

Bottom-Up Weight Adjustments

The weight adjustment formula (Equation 8-6, repeated here for reference) is central to the operation of the ART system.

$$b_{ij} = (L\, c_i)/\left(L - 1 + \sum_k c_k\right) \qquad (8\text{-}6)$$

The summation in the denominator represents the number of ones in the output of the comparison layer. As such, this number may be thought of as the "size" of this vector. With this interpretation, large **C** vectors produce smaller weight values for b_{ij} than do small **C** vectors. This "self-scaling" property makes it possible to separate two vectors when one is a subset of another; that is, its ones are in some but not all of the positions of the other.

To demonstrate the problem that results if the scaling shown in Equation 8-6 is not used, suppose that the network has been trained on the two input vectors that follow, with a recognition-layer neuron assigned to each.

$$\mathbf{X}_1 = 1\ 0\ 0\ 0\ 0$$

$$\mathbf{X}_2 = 1\ 1\ 1\ 0\ 0$$

Note that $\mathbf{X}_1$ is a subset of $\mathbf{X}_2$. Without the scaling property, bottom-up weights would be trained to the same values for each pattern. If this value were chosen to be 1.0, the weight patterns that follow would result.

$$\mathbf{T}_1 = \mathbf{B}_1 = 1\ 0\ 0\ 0\ 0$$

$$\mathbf{T}_2 = \mathbf{B}_2 = 1\ 1\ 1\ 0\ 0$$

If $\mathbf{X}_1$ is applied once more, both recognition-layer neurons receive the same activation; hence, likely as not, neuron 2, the wrong one, will win the competition.

In addition to making an incorrect classification, training can be destroyed. Because $\mathbf{T}_2$ feeds down 1 1 1 0 0, only the first 1 is matched by the input vector, $\mathbf{C}$ becomes 1 0 0 0 0, vigilance is satisfied, and training sets the second and third 1s of $\mathbf{T}_2$ and $\mathbf{B}_2$ to 0, destroying the trained pattern.

Scaling the bottom-up weights according to Equation 8-6 prevents this undesirable behavior. Suppose, for example, that Equation 8-6 is used with $L = 2$, thereby producing the formula that follows:

$$b_{ij} = (2\ c_i)/\left(1 + \sum_k c_k\right)$$

Bottom-up weights will now train to the values

$$\mathbf{B}_1 = 1\quad 0\quad 0\quad 0\ 0$$

$$\mathbf{B}_2 = {}^1/_2\ {}^1/_2\ {}^1/_2\ 0\ 0$$

Applying $\mathbf{X}_1$ produces an excitation of 1.0 on recognition-layer neuron 1, but only 1/2 for neuron 2; thus, neuron 1 (correctly) wins the competition. Similarly, applying $\mathbf{X}_2$ produces excitation levels of 1.0 for neuron 1, but 3/2 for neuron 2, again selecting the correct winner.

Bottom-Up Weight Initialization

Initializing the bottom-up weights to low values is essential to the correct functioning of the ART system. If they are too high, input vectors that have already been learned will activate an uncommitted recognition-layer neuron rather than the one that has been previously trained. The formula for bottom-up weight assignments, Equation 8-1, is repeated here for reference:

$$b_{ij} < L/(L - 1 + m) \quad \text{for all } i, j \qquad (8\text{-}1)$$

Setting these weights to low values ensures that an uncommitted neuron will not "overpower" a trained recognition-layer neuron. Using our previous example with $L = 2$ and $m = 5$, $b_{ij} < 1/3$, so we arbitrarily set $b_{ij} = 1/6$. With these weights, applying a vector for which the network has been trained will cause the correctly trained recognition-layer neuron to win over an uncommitted neuron. For example, on an uncommitted neuron, X_1 would produce an excitation of 1/6, while X_2 would produce 1/2; both are below the excitation produced on the neuron for which they were trained.

Searching

It may appear that direct access obviates the need for a search except when an uncommitted recognition-layer neuron is to be assigned. This is not the case; application of an input vector that is similar, but not identical, to one of the stored patterns may not on the first trial select a recognition-layer neuron such that the similarity S exceeds the vigilance ρ, even though another neuron will.

As in the preceding example, assume that the network has been trained on the two vectors that follow:

$$\mathbf{X}_1 = 1\ 0\ 0\ 0\ 0$$

$$\mathbf{X}_2 = 1\ 1\ 1\ 0\ 0$$

with bottom-up weight vectors trained as follows:

$$\mathbf{B}_1 = 1\quad 0\quad 0\quad 0\ 0$$

$$\mathbf{B}_2 = 1/2\ \ 1/2\ \ 1/2\ 0\ 0$$

Now apply an input vector $\mathbf{X}_3 = 1\ 1\ 0\ 0\ 0$. In this case, the excitation to recognition-layer neuron 1 will be 1.0, while that of neuron 2 will be only 2/3. Neuron 1 will win (even though it is not the best match), $\mathbf{C}$ will be set to 1 0 0 0 0, and the similarity S will be 1/2. If the vigilance is set at 3/4, neuron 1 will be disabled, and neuron 2 will now win the competition. $\mathbf{C}$ will now become 1 1 0 0 0, S will be 1, the vigilance will be satisfied, and the search will stop.

Theorems of ART

In Carpenter and Grossberg (1987a), several theorems are proven that show powerful characteristics to be inherent to the system. The four results that follow are among the most important:

1. After training has stabilized, application of one of the training vectors (or one with the essential features of the category) will activate the correct recognition-layer neuron without searching. This "direct-access" characteristic implies rapid access to previously learned patterns.

2. The search process is stable. After the winning recognition-layer neuron is chosen, the system will not switch from one neuron to another as a result of the top-down vector's modification of **C**, the output of the comparison layer; only reset can cause this change.

3. Similarly, training is stable. Training will not cause a switch from one recognition-layer neuron to another.

4. The training process terminates. Any sequence of arbitrary input vectors will produce a stable set of weights after a finite number of learning trials; no repetitive sequence of training vectors will cause ART's weights to cycle endlessly.

DISCUSSION

ART is an interesting and important paradigm. It solves the stability–plasticity dilemma and performs well in other regards. The ART architecture was designed to be biologically plausible; that is, its mechanisms are intended to be consistent with those of the brain (as we understand them). It may fail, however, to simulate the distributed storage of internal representations, which many see as an important characteristic of the cerebral function. ART's exemplars represent "grandmother cells"; loss of one cell destroys an entire memory. In contrast, memories in the brain seem to be distributed over substantial regions; a recollection can often survive considerable physical damage without being lost entirely.

It seems logical to study architectures that do not violate our understanding of the brain's organization and function. The human brain constitutes an existence proof that a solution to the pattern-recognition problem is possible. It seems sensible to emulate this working system if we wish to duplicate its performance. However, a counterargument recounts the history of powered flight; man failed to get off the ground until he stopped trying to imitate the moving wings and feathers of the birds.

References

Carpenter, G., and Grossberg, S. 1986. Neural dynamics of category learning and recognition: Attention, memory consolidation, and amnesia. In *Brain Structure, Learning and Memory* (AAAS Symposium Series), eds. J. Davis., R. Newburgh, and E. Wegman.

_____. 1987a. A massively parallel architecture for a self-organizing neural pattern recognition machine. *Computer Vision, Graphics, and Image Processing* 37:54–115.

_____. 1987b. ART 2: Self-organization of stable category recognition codes for analog input patterns. *Applied Optics* 26(23):4919–30.

Grossberg, S. 1987. Competitive learning: From interactive activation to adaptive resonance. *Cognitive Science* 11:23–63.

Lippman, R. P. 1987. An introduction to computing with neural nets. *IEEE Transactions on Acoustics, Speech and Signal Processing*, April, pp. 4–22.

9

Optical Neural Networks

Neural network use and training require two types of operations: computation and communication. Computational functions are performed easily and well by electronic systems. Integrated-circuit logic elements operate in nanoseconds. In addition, they have dimensions measured in microns and can be manufactured for less than a hundredth of a cent per gate.

Communication tasks are not so easily performed. Electronic signals in integrated circuits require conductors from gate to gate. Although these conductors are only microns wide, the space they require (and the spaces required to insulate one from another) can become so large that there is insufficient silicon area left for the circuits that perform the computation. Although techniques have been devised to partition circuits for ordinary digital computers so that large functional blocks are interconnected with relatively few conductors, these techniques break down in the face of massive parallelism. Similarly, no such solution is presently known for artificial neural networks. The power of these systems comes specifically from their high connectivity; taken individually, the computational elements have little ability.

Achieving the needed connectivity in electronic circuits poses serious problems. Carver Mead (1988) has conjectured that the density of conductors in a two-dimensional system must decrease inversely as the square of the distance from the source neuron; otherwise, there is no possibility of producing the system on an integrated circuit. This is an unrealistic restriction with today's networks that emphasize full interconnection.

Optical neural networks promise a way out of this dilemma. By interconnecting neurons with light beams, no insulation is required between signal paths; light rays can pass through each other without interacting. Furthermore, the signal paths can be made in three dimensions. (Integrated circuits are essentially planar, with some relief provided by multiple layers.) Also, the transmission-path density is limited only by the spacing of light sources, their divergence, and the spacing of the detectors—potentially, a distance of a few microns. Finally, all signal paths can be operating simultaneously, thereby producing a truly prodigious data rate. The result of these characteristics is a system capable of achieving full connectivity, all at the speed of light.

Optical neural networks can also provide important computational benefits. Strengths of synaptic connections can be stored in holograms with high density; some estimates place the theoretical limit as high as 10^{12} bits per cubic centimeter. While such estimates have not yet been approached in practice, the potential exists for extremely high levels of storage density. Furthermore, these weights can be modified during operation to produce a fully adaptive system.

Given all of these advantages, one might be expected to ask why anyone would make a network in any other way. Unfortunately, there are many practical problems with optical implementations. Optical devices have their own physical characteristics, and they often do not match up well with the requirements of artificial neural networks. Although they are naturally suited to image processing, the images from optical neural networks to date have been disappointingly poor. Still, one need only view the early attempts at television images to see that enormous improvements in image quality are possible. Despite such problems as cost, size, and criticalness of alignment, the potential of optical systems has motivated (and is motivating) intensive and extensive research efforts. Major improvements are expected and eagerly awaited.

The many optical neural network configurations being studied may be divided into only two categories: vector-matrix multipliers and holographic correlators. An example of each is presented in this chapter. However, a detailed treatment of optical physics is beyond the scope of this volume. Instead, qualitative explanations of the overall operation are provided, and the author's view of likely developments in the field is presented.

VECTOR-MATRIX MULTIPLIERS

The operation of most artificial neural networks can be described mathematically as a series of vector-matrix multiplications, one for each layer. To calculate the output of a layer, an input vector is applied and then multiplied by the weight matrix to produce the NET vector. This vector is then operated on by the activation function F to produce the OUT vector for that layer. In symbols

$$NET = \mathbf{XW}$$

$$OUT = F(NET)$$

where
  NET = the row vector formed from weighted sums of inputs
  OUT = the output row vector
  $\mathbf{X}$ = the input row vector
  $\mathbf{W}$ = the weight matrix

In biological neural networks, this operation is performed by large numbers of neurons operating simultaneously; hence, the system responds rapidly despite the slowness of each neuron.

When artificial neural networks are simulated on general-purpose computers, the inherently parallel nature of the computation is lost; each operation must be performed sequentially. Despite the rapidity of individual computations, the number of operations required for the matrix multiplication is proportional to the square of the size of the input vector (for input and output vectors of equal size), and computation time can become intolerably long.

Electro-Optical Matrix Multipliers

Electro-optical neural nets provide a means for performing matrix multiplication in parallel. Studied by Farhat, Psaltis, Prata, and

Paek (1985), Fisher, Giles, and Lee (1985), and Athale, Friedlander, and Kushner (1986), such networks perform at speeds limited only by available electro-optical components; computation times are potentially in the subnanosecond range.

Figure 9-1 shows a system capable of multiplying a six-element input vector by a six-by-five matrix, producing a five-element NET vector. On the right, a column of light sources passes its rays through a cylindrical lens; each light uniformly illuminates a single row of the weight mask. Thus, light 1 illuminates w_{11}, w_{12}, w_{15}. The weight mask may be a photographic film in which the transmittance of each square is proportional to the weight. On the left side is a second cylindrical lens that focuses the light from each column of the mask onto a corresponding photodetector.

Thus, the light impinging on photodetector 1 is the sum of the products of the light intensities multiplied by the transmittances for column 1. Symbolically,

$$\text{NET}_j = \sum_i W_{ij} X_i$$

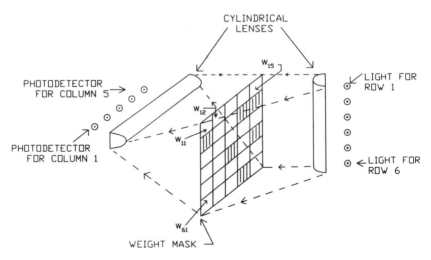

Figure 9-1. Electro-Optical Vector-Matrix Multiplier

where

NET$_j$ = the NET output of neuron j (output of photodetector j)

W_{ij} = the weight from neuron i to neuron j (transmittance of the weight mask at row i, column j)

X_i = the input vector component i (output of light source i)

Each photodetector output represents the dot product between the input vector and a column of the weight matrix. Therefore, the set of outputs is a vector equal to the product of the input vector with the weight matrix.

This matrix multiplication is performed in parallel. With suitable high-speed light-emitting diodes and PIN photodetectors, the entire vector-matrix multiplication can take place in less than a nanosecond. Furthermore, speed is largely independent of the size of the array. This allows networks to be scaled up without materially increasing the time required for computation. In this simple version, the weights are fixed; they can only be changed by substituting a different weight mask. To be useful in an adaptive system, the weights must be variable. One promising method uses a liquid crystal light valve in place of the photographic negative. This permits the weights to be adjusted electronically in tens of microseconds. At present, the liquid-crystal light valve is suitable for binary weights, but lacks the stability and contrast needed for continuously variable weights. This is a situation that may change in the near future.

Hopfield Net Using Electro-Optical Matrix Multipliers

If the photodetector outputs of the network are fed back to drive the corresponding light inputs, an electro-optical Hopfield net is produced. To do so, a threshold activation function must be provided. Today, this is best done in electronics circuitry following each photodetector.

To satisfy the stability requirements, the weight array must be symmetrical with transmittance set to zero for squares on the main diagonal (w_{11}, w_{12}, . . . , w_{mn}).

Electro-Optical Bidirectional Associative Memories (BAMs)

If two of the systems in Figure 9-1 are cascaded (the outputs of the second system feeding back to the inputs of the first), an electro-optical BAM is produced. To ensure stability, the second weight mask must be the transpose of the first.

Kosko (1987) has described a compact system in which only a single mask and optical system is required (see Figure 9-2). Here, each photodetector and light source is replaced by a photodetector-light source pair. The operation is similar to that described for the simple photo-optical multiplier, except that the output from each photodetector drives its adjacent light source.

In operation, light from each light source on the right passes through the cylindrical lens, illuminating the corresponding row of the weight mask. These lenses act to spread the light in a horizontal direction, while leaving it collimated in the vertical direction.

On the left, each photodetector receives all of the light from a column of the weight mask, and its electronics provide the threshold function to produce the NET output. The output of the electronics then drives the adjacent left-side light source, the light from which passes through the optics to illuminate the same column. It may be seen that the same space in the optics is occupied

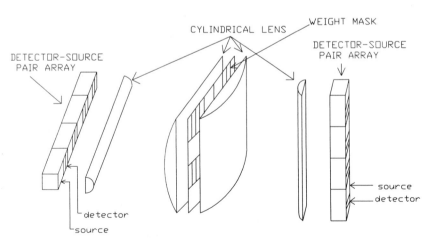

Figure 9-2.   Electro-Optical Bidirectional Associative Memory

by light patterns passing from left to right and from right to left. Since light rays do not interact, this causes no problems.

On the right side, each photodetector responds to the light from an entire row, and its electronics perform the threshold function and drive the adjacent light source. In this way, a feedback loop is closed, coupling light sources, photodetectors, and the optical system. Note that BAM stability is ensured even if the matrix is not symmetrical; also, the main diagonal need not be zero.

Linear Modulator Arrays

The linear modulator, a device currently under development, promises to simplify substantially the structure of electro-optical networks. As shown in Figure 9-3, it consists of a thin plate with alternate stripes of light-sensing material and optical modulators. The transmissivity of each stripe of the optical modulator region can be varied electronically.

Figure 9-4 shows a simplified linear modulator assembly used as an optical matrix multiplier. The horizontal optical modulator stripes are electronically controlled. The transmissivity of each stripe corresponds to the magnitude of a component of the **X** input vector, thereby controlling the amount of light impinging upon the corresponding row of the weight mask. In this system, there are no separate lights for each row; one collimated source of light enters from the right and passes through each modulator stripe onto the weight mask. Light passing through the weight mask falls onto the vertical light-sensing columns. Each column produces an output proportional to the total light passing through a corresponding column of the weight mask. Thus, the effect is identical to that previously described for a lens system that concentrates light onto a small photodetector; this system performs matrix multiplication with precisely the same results.

Because the linear modulator array passes collimated light, no cylindrical lenses are required. This solves the difficult problem of geometric distortion associated with the optics of earlier designs. The advantages of compact construction and optical simplicity are somewhat offset by the relatively slow speed of operation; current technology requires tens of microseconds to switch the light modulators.

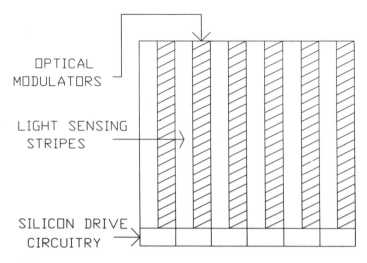

Figure 9-3.   Linear Spatial-Light Modulator Array

BAM Implementation Using Linear Modulator Arrays

Figure 9-5 shows a BAM constructed with linear modulator arrays. It is similar to the multiplier described above, except that each column light-detector stripe on the left drives a threshold circuit, which in turn controls the transmissivity of its adjacent vertical stripe. In this way, a second collimated light source from the left is

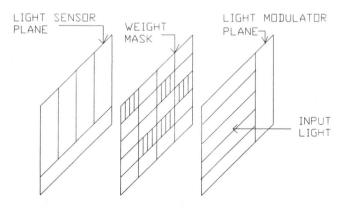

Figure 9-4.   Linear Modulator Used as an Optical Matrix Multiplier

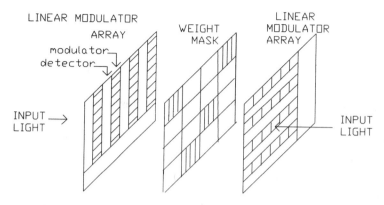

Figure 9-5. Optical Bidirectional Associative Memory Using Linear Modulator Arrays

modulated, and the corresponding column of the weight mask receives a controlled illumination level. This produces the necessary feedback signal to the horizontal rows of light detectors on the right; their output signals are thresholded and control the transmissivity of their corresponding horizontal light-modulator stripes, thereby closing the BAM feedback loop.

HOLOGRAPHIC CORRELATORS

Although there are many variations of the holographic correlator, their fundamental operating principles are quite similar. They all store reference images in either a thin or volume hologram and retrieve them in a coherently illuminated feedback loop. An input image, which may be noisy or incomplete, is applied to the system and is simultaneously correlated optically with all of the stored reference images. These correlations are thresholded and fed back to the input, where the strongest correlation reinforces (and possibly corrects or completes) the input image. The enhanced image passes around the loop repeatedly, approaching the stored image more closely on each pass, until the system stabilizes on the desired image. Note that the term "image" has been used to describe the pattern being recognized. Although image recognition is the most common application for the optical correlator, the input can be treated as a generalized vector and the system becomes a general-purpose associative memory.

Many researchers have made major contributions to the holographic correlator and its underlying theory. For example, Dunning, Marom, Owechko, and Soffer (1985), Jannson, Karagaleff, and Stoll (1986), and Anderson (1985) have all done excellent research. Abu-Mostafa and Psaltis (1987) have demonstrated an impressive system that serves as the basis for the discussion that follows.

In the configuration shown in Figure 9-6, the input to the system is an image formed by illuminating a transparency with a laser beam. This image is applied to a beam splitter, which passes it to the threshold device, the function of which is discussed below. The image is reflected from the threshold device, passed back to the beam splitter, and then to lens 1, which focuses it onto the first hologram.

The first hologram contains several stored images (perhaps images of four aircraft). The image is correlated with each of them, producing patterns of light. The brightness of these patterns varies with the degree of correlation, a measure of the similarity between the two images. Lens 2 and mirror 1 project these image correlations onto a pinhole array, where they are spatially separated. From

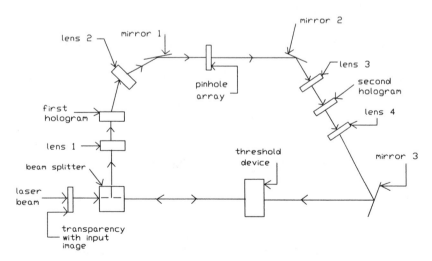

Figure 9-6.   Optical Image-Recognition System

the pinhole array, the multiple light patterns pass to mirror 2, through lens 3, and then are applied to the second hologram, which has the same stored images as the first hologram. Lens 4 and mirror 3 then produce a superposition of the multiple correlated images onto the back side of the threshold device.

The threshold device is the key to the operation of this system. Its front surface reflects most strongly that pattern that is brightest on its rear surface. In this case, its rear surface has projected on it the set of four correlations of each of the four stored images with the input image. The stored image most like the input image has the highest correlation; hence, it is the brightest and will be most strongly reflected from the front surface. This reinforced reflected image goes through the beam splitter, where it re-enters the loop for further enhancement. Eventually, the system will converge on the stored pattern most like the input pattern. At this point, the input pattern may be removed and the stored pattern will continue to "reverberate" around the loop, producing the same output image until it is reset.

Videotaped demonstrations of this system show it completing an image when only a fraction of the image is applied to the system. This has important military significance because target recognition often must be performed under conditions of partial visibility. Also, many industrial applications are possible; recognizing objects on an assembly line is a perennial problem.

Despite the exciting potential for optical correlators, the image quality of existing systems is low and their complexity and cost are high. In addition, at present they are bulky and difficult to align. The tremendous application potential will motivate improvements in performance; however, many questions remain unanswered regarding their ultimate practicality.

Volume Holograms

Certain crystals (Jannson, Karagaleff, and Stoll 1986) will bend an incident light beam; the amount of bending can be modified by a laser. If neurons are designed to both receive and transmit light, these photorefractive crystals can be used to interconnect large networks. Psaltis, Wagner, and Brady (1987) have studied the potential density of such interconnective systems and estimate that from 10^8 to 10^{10} interconnections per cubic centimeter are possible.

The amount and direction in which a light beam is bent by a photorefractive crystal are determined by internal holographic gratings formed by a high-intensity laser beam. The crystal's local index of refraction is a function of its local charge density. The laser redistributes the charge by dislocating electrons, thus forming regions of varying refracting power. If a light ray connecting a pair of neurons impinges on the crystal at an appropriate point, it will be bent (refracted) by the proper angle to direct it to the destination neuron.

Furthermore, the strength of each grating can be controlled as it is written by the laser beam, thereby varying the percentage of the incident beam that is refracted. This effectively changes the weight of the interconnections, allowing the system weights to be modified by a learning algorithm.

An Optical Hopfield Net Using Volume Holograms

An all-optical recurrent neural network using volume holograms has been reported by Stoll and Lee (1988). It operates as an implementation of the Hopfield net, seeking a minimum on an optically generated energy surface. When a noisy or incomplete input pattern is applied, the system converges to the stored image that is most similar, thereby functioning as an optical associative memory.

Figure 9-7 is a simplified configuration of the system. A resonant loop encloses the optical neuron array, the optical interconnect matrix, and the associated optical components. Images (represented as vectors) pass around this feedback loop in the direction indicated by the arrows, being amplified in the process. There is a close analogy here to the operation of the Hopfield network. The optical neuron array sums the input and the feedback signals, and then applies the sigmoidal activation function; the optical interconnect matrix performs the vector-matrix multiplication.

When an input vector (perhaps representing an image) is applied at the right, it passes through beam splitter BS_2 to the optical neu-

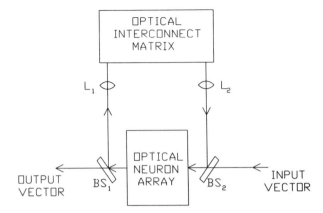

Figure 9-7. Optical Hopfield Network

ron array. Here it is amplified, and a sigmoidal function is applied by a saturating two-beam amplifier. The "squashed" output vector is partially reflected by beam splitter BS_1 to lens L_1, where it enters the optical interconnect matrix. A portion of the output light also passes through BS_1 and constitutes the system output.

The optical interconnect matrix consists of two volume holograms that store the reference images as diffraction patterns written by laser beams. These serve to weight the input components and direct each weighted sum to the correct element of the optical output vector.

The Optical Neuron

Figure 9-8 shows the construction of a typical element in the optical neuron array. It operates as an optically pumped, two-beam saturating amplifier in a crystal of $BaTiO_3$ (Fainman, Klancnik, and Lee 1986). A laser pump beam applied at an angle θ interacts with the input beam to produce an amplified replica of the input, with the familiar sigmoidal activation function applied (see Figure 9-9). An optical gain of approximately sixty has been achieved through this technique. Note in Figure 9-8 that the angle ϕ between the input beam and the crystalline C axis is critical to the correct functioning of this device.

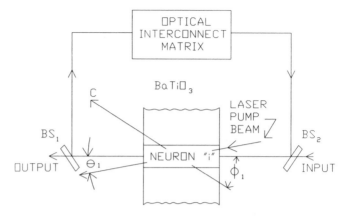

Figure 9-8.   Optical Neuron Array

Optical Interconnect Matrix

In the optical interconnect matrix, the signal from the optical neuron array passes into an optical system containing two volume holograms. The optical Fourier transform of the input is first produced using standard Fourier optics techniques. Then this is applied to the first volume hologram, where the reference vectors are stored in phase-encoded Fourier space. The output of this holo-

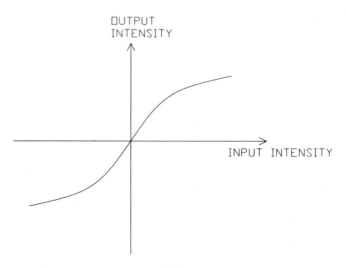

Figure 9-9.   Sigmoidal Activation Function

gram is applied to a two-beam optical amplifier similar to that of the optical neuron, but operated in a nonsaturating mode. This raises the gain to the point at which loop regeneration is possible. The inverse Fourier transform of the amplified output is then produced optically and applied to the second volume hologram, where the same reference images are stored, this time in object space (rather than phase-encoded Fourier space). The output of the system is then the superposition of the vector-matrix products between the input vector and the stored reference vectors. This optical pattern emerges from the optical interconnect matrix and is applied to the optical neuron array to close the feedback loop.

This discussion of the optical interconnect matrix is greatly simplified; the implementation details involve sophisticated optical processing techniques that are beyond the scope of this volume. Interested readers are referred to Stoll and Lee (1988), as well as to Fainman, Klancnik, and Lee (1986).

DISCUSSION

Optical neural networks offer tremendous advantages in speed and interconnect density. They can be used (in one form or another) to implement virtually any network architecture, including backpropagation (Psaltis, Wagner, and Brady 1987).

Today, limitations in electro-optical devices create a number of vexing problems that must be solved before optical neural nets can find widespread application. However, considering the number of excellent researchers who are working on this problem and the large military backing, rapid progress may be expected.

References

Abu-Mostafa, Y. S., and Psaltis D. 1987. Optical neural computers. *Scientific American*, March, pp. 88–95.

Anderson, D. Z. 1985. Coherent optical Eigenstate memory. *Proceedings of the Optical Society of America 1985 Annual Meeting*.

Athale, R. A., Friedlander, C. B., and Kushner, C. B. 1986. Attentive associative architectures and their implications to optical computing. *Proceedings of the Society of Photo-Optical Instrumentation Engineering* 625:179–88.

Dunning, G. J., Marom, E., Owechko, Y., and Soffer, B. H. 1985. All-optical associative holographic memory with feedback using phase conjugate mirrors. *Proceedings of the Society of Photo-Optical Instrumentation Engineering* 625:179–188.

Fainman, Y., Klancnik, E., and Lee, S. H. 1986. *Optical Engineering* 25:228.

Farhat, N. H., Psaltis, D., Prata, A., and Paek, E. 1985. Optical implementation of the Hopfield model. *Applied Optics* 24:1469–75.

Fisher, A. D., Giles, C. L., and Lee, J. N. 1985. An adaptive optical computing element. *Proceedings of the Optical Society of America Topical Meeting*.

Jannson, T., Karagaleff, C., and Stoll, H. M. 1986. Photorefractive $LiNbO_3$ as a storage medium for high-density optical neural networks. *1986 Optical Society of America Annual Meeting*.

Kosko, B. 1987. Optical bidirectional associative memories. *Proceedings of the Society of Photo-Optical Instrumentation Engineering: Image Understanding and the Man–Machine Interface* 758:11–18.

Mead, C. 1988. Paper presented during plenary session. *IEEE Second International Conference on Neural Networks*. San Diego, June.

Psaltis, D., Wagner, K., and Brady, D. 1987. Learning in optical neural computers. In *Proceedings of IEEE First International Conference on Neural Networks*, eds. M. Caudill and C. Butler. San Diego, CA: SOS Printing.

Stoll, H. M., and Lee, L. S. 1988. Continuous time optical neural network. *Proceedings of IEEE International Conference on Neural Networks*. San Diego, CA: SOS Printing.

10

The Cognitron and Neocognitron

Humans perform complex pattern-recognition tasks with disarming ease. Watch a two-year-old. With no apparent effort, the toddler recognizes thousands of faces and objects in his environment, doing so despite variations in distance, rotation, translation, perspective, and illumination.

It would seem that all of this innate talent should make it simple for humans to produce computers that duplicate these recognition skills. Nothing could be further from the truth. Pattern differences and similarities that are obvious to a human still confound the most sophisticated computer pattern-recognition systems. Thus, innumerable important applications in which computers might replace humans in dangerous, dull, or unpleasant tasks remain beyond their current capabilities.

Computer pattern recognition is largely an art; the science is limited to a few techniques, with little to direct their application. An engineer designing a typical computer pattern-recognition system usually starts with textbook techniques. These are often found inadequate, and the effort quickly shifts to ad hoc algorithms specific to the task at hand.

The usual objective of a pattern-recognition system design is to optimize performance over a sample set of patterns. Too often, the designer completes this task only to find a new, superficially similar pattern that causes the algorithms to fail. This process can continue indefinitely, never producing a solution robust enough to duplicate the perceptions of the human who is evaluating its performance.

Fortunately, we have an existence proof that the task can be done: the human perceptual system. With the limited success achieved in pursuing our own inventions, it seems logical to return to the biological model and try to determine how it functions so well. This has proven difficult for several reasons. First, the brain's extraordinary complexity obscures its operating principles. With roughly 10^{11} neurons and 10^{14} synaptic connections, its overall principles of operation have been difficult to discern. Also, experimental problems abound. Microscopic examination requires elaborate sample preparation (freezing, slicing, staining, etc.) to yield a small two-dimensional view of a large three-dimensional structure. Microprobe techniques allow measurements of the internal cell electrochemistry, but it has proven difficult to monitor simultaneously a large number of cells and observe their patterns of interaction. Finally, ethical considerations prohibit many important experiments that can be performed only on humans. A great deal has been learned from animal experiments, but there is no substitute for the ability of the human to report perceptions.

Despite these limitations, a great deal has been learned through brilliantly conceived experiments. For example, Blakemore and Cooper (1970) describe an experiment in which kittens were raised in a visual environment consisting only of horizontal black and white stripes. It is known that certain areas of the visual cortex are sensitive to edge orientation, yet these cats developed no cortical neurons sensitive to vertical stripes. This result strongly suggests that the mammalian brain does not come fully "prewired," even at the primitive level of recognizing line orientation. Instead, it self-organizes based upon experience.

At a microscopic level, neurons have been found to possess both excitatory and inhibitory synapses. The former tend to cause the neuron to fire; the latter suppress its firing (see Appendix A). This suggests that the brain adapts either by adjusting the efficiency of these synapses or by creating and/or destroying synapses as a result of environmental stimulation. This remains a hypothesis with limited physiological confirmation. Yet it has inspired the creation of numerous models, some of which exhibit remarkably brainlike adaptive pattern-recognition capabilities.

THE COGNITRON

Building on current knowledge of brain anatomy and physiology, Fukushima (1975) has developed the cognitron, a hypothetical mathematical model of the human perceptual system. His computer simulations have demonstrated impressive adaptive pattern-recognition capabilities, motivating physiologists to search for corresponding brain mechanisms. This mutually reinforcing interplay between artificial neural networks, physiology, and psychology may be the means by which an understanding of the brain is eventually achieved.

Structure

The cognitron is constructed of layers of neurons connected by synapses. As shown in Figure 10-1, a presynaptic neuron in one layer feeds a postsynaptic neuron in the next layer. There are two types of neurons: excitatory cells, which tend to cause the postsynaptic cell to fire, and inhibitory cells, which reduce this tenden-

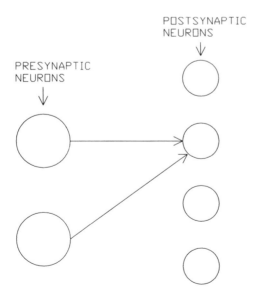

Figure 10-1.   Presynaptic and Postsynaptic Neurons

cy. The firing of a neuron depends upon the weighted sums of its excitatory and inhibitory inputs; however, the actual mechanism is somewhat more complex than simple summation.

Figure 10-2 shows that each neuron connects only to neurons in the nearby area, called its *connection region*. This limited range is consistent with the anatomy of the visual cortex, where connections are seldom made between neurons further than one millimeter apart. In Fukushima's model, neurons are arranged in layers, with the connections from one layer going to the next. Again, this is like the layered structure of the visual cortex, as well as other portions of the brain.

Training

Because Fukushima implemented the cognitron as a multilayer network, he was obliged to face the perplexing training problems associated with this structure. He rejected supervised training as biologically implausible, using instead an algorithm that trains without a teacher. Given a training set of input patterns, the network self-organizes by adjusting its synaptic strengths. There are no predetermined output patterns representing the desired re-

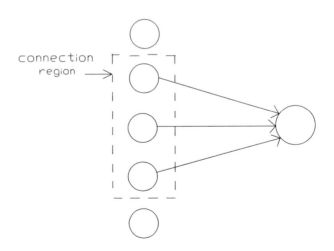

Figure 10-2. Connection Region of a Neuron

sponse, yet the network adjusts itself to recognize patterns on its input with remarkable accuracy.

The cognitron training algorithm is conceptually appealing. In a given region of a layer, only the most vigorously firing neuron is trained. Fukushima likens this to "elite education," in that only the most knowledgeable cells receive training. Those that are already well trained, as shown by the strength of their firing, have their synaptic strengths increased to further enhance their firing.

Note in Figure 10-3 that the connection regions of nearby cells have considerable overlap; thus, there is a tendency for groups of cells to have similar response patterns. This wasteful duplication of function is avoided by incorporating competition among nearby cells. Even if cells start out to have identical responses, minor variations will occur; one cell in a competition region will usually respond more strongly than its neighbors to an input pattern. Its vigorous firing will act to suppress the firing of nearby cells, and only its synapses will be reinforced; those of its neighbors will remain unchanged.

The Excitatory Neuron

Roughly speaking, the output of the excitatory cognitron neuron is determined by the ratio of its excitatory inputs to inhibitory inputs. This unusual function has significant advantages, both practical and theoretical.

The total excitatory input to a neuron E is simply the weighted sum of the inputs from the excitatory neurons in the previous layer. Similarly, the total inhibitory input I is the weighted sum of the inputs from the inhibitory neurons. In symbols

$$E = \sum_i a_i u_i$$

$$I = \sum_j b_j v_j$$

where

a_i = the weight of the ith excitatory synapse
u_i = the output from the ith excitatory neuron
b_j = the weight of the ith inhibitory synapse

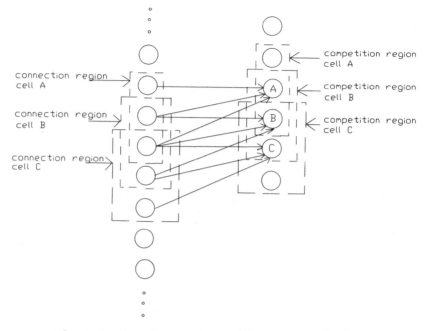

Figure 10-3.   Connection and Competition Regions

v_j = the output from the ith inhibitory neuron

Note that weights take on only positive values.
  The output of a neuron is then calculated as follows:

$$\text{NET} = [(1 + E)/(1 + I)] - 1$$
$$\text{OUT} = \text{NET for NET} > = 0$$
$$\text{OUT} = 0 \text{ for NET} < 0$$

Assuming positive values for NET, this may be rewritten as:

$$\text{OUT} = (E - I)/(1 + I)$$

When the inhibitory input is small ($I \ll 1$), OUT can be approximated as OUT = $E - I$, which agrees with the formula for a conventional linear threshold element (with a threshold of zero).
  The cognitron training algorithm allows the synaptic strengths

to increase without bound. Because there is no mechanism to reduce a weight, they simply increase throughout the training process. In a conventional linear threshold element, this would result in an arbitrarily large output. In the cognitron, large excitatory and inhibitory inputs result in the limiting formula that follows:

$$\text{OUT} = (E/I) - 1 \text{ if } E \gg 1 \text{ and } I \gg 1$$

In this case, OUT is determined by the ratio of the excitatory inputs to inhibitory inputs, rather than by their difference. Thus, the value of OUT is limited, provided that both types of input increase at the same rate X. Given that this is true, E and I can be expressed as follows:

$$E = pX$$

$$I = qX$$

$$p, q = \text{constants}$$

and with some transformations,

$$\text{OUT} = [(p - q)/2q]\{1 + \tanh [\log (pq)/2]\}$$

This function agrees with the Weber-Fechner law, an expression often used in neurophysiology to approximate the nonlinear input/output relations of sensory neurons. By utilizing this relationship, the cognitron neuron closely emulates the responses of the biological neuron. This makes it both a powerful computational element and an accurate model for physiological simulations.

The Inhibitory Neuron

In the cognitron, a layer consists of both excitatory and inhibitory cells. As shown in Figure 10-4, a layer 2 neuron has a connection region over which it has synaptic connections to a set of layer 1 neuron outputs. Similarly, in layer 1, there is an inhibitory neuron with the same connection region. Synaptic weights coming into inhibitory cells are not modified during training; their weights are preselected so that the sum of the weights into any inhibitory neuron is equal to one. With this restriction, the output of the

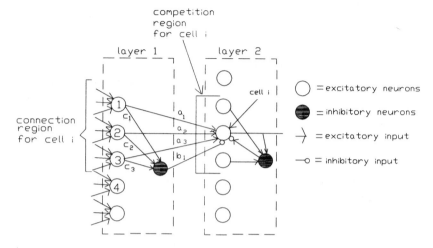

Figure 10-4. Cognitron Layers

inhibitory cell INHIB is simply the weighted sum of its inputs, which in this case is the arithmetic mean of the excitatory outputs to which it connects. Hence,

$$INHIB = \sum_i c_i\, OUT_i$$

where

$$\sum_i c_i = 1$$

c_i = inhibitory weight i

Training Procedure

As previously explained, the weights associated with an excitatory neuron are adjusted only when it is firing more strongly than any of the neighboring cells in its competition region. When this is so, the change in one of its weights is calculated as follows:

$$\delta\, a_i = q\, c_j\, u_j$$

where

c_j = the inhibitory weight coming from neuron j in layer 1 to the inhibitory neuron i

u_j = the output of neuron j in layer 1
a_i = excitatory weight i
q = the learning rate coefficient

The change in the inhibitory weight into neuron i in layer 2 is proportional to the ratio of the weighted sum of excitatory inputs to twice the inhibitory input. This is calculated by the formula

$$\delta b_i = q\left(\sum_j a_j u_j\right)/(2\ \text{INHIB}_i)$$

When no neurons fire in a competition region, somewhat different weight adjustment formulas are used. This is necessary because the training process starts with all weights set to zero; thus, initially no neurons fire in any competition region and training cannot occur. In all cases in which there is no winner in a neuron's competition region, its weight changes are calculated as follows:

$$\delta a_i = q'\,c_j\,u_j$$

$$\delta b_i = q'\,\text{INHIB}_i$$

where q' is a positive training coefficient less than q.

This adjustment strategy ensures that a cell with a large response causes the excitatory synapses that it drives to increase more than the inhibitory synapses. Conversely, cells having a small output make small increases in the excitatory synapses, but larger increases in the inhibitory synapses. Thus, if cell 1 in layer 1 has a large output, synapse a_1 increases more than synapse b_1. Conversely, cells having only a small output produce small values for a_i. But other cells in the connection region will be firing, thereby raising the INHIB signal and increasing b_i.

Training adjusts the weights of each layer 2 cell so that together they constitute a template conforming to patterns that the cell saw frequently during the training process. Presented with a familiar pattern, the template is matched and the cell produces a large output. Unfamiliar patterns produce a small output, which is usually suppressed by competition.

Lateral Inhibition.   In Figure 10-4, each layer 2 neuron is shown to receive lateral inhibition from neurons in its competition region.

An inhibitory neuron sums inputs from all neurons in the competition region and outputs a signal that tends to inhibit the target neuron. This method is functional, but computationally slow. It comprises a large feedback system involving every neuron in a layer; many computational iterations are required for it to stabilize.

To accelerate calculations, Fukushima uses an ingenious method of forward lateral inhibition (see Figure 10-5). Here, an additional lateral inhibition cell processes the output of each excitatory cell to simulate the desired lateral inhibition. First, it defines a signal equal to the total inhibitory influence in a competition region as follows:

$$\text{LAT\_INHIB} = \sum_i g_i \, \text{OUT}_i$$

where

    OUT_i = the output of the ith neuron in a competition region

      g_i = the weight from that neuron to the lateral-inhibition neuron

and g_i is chosen so that $\sum_i g_i = 1$.

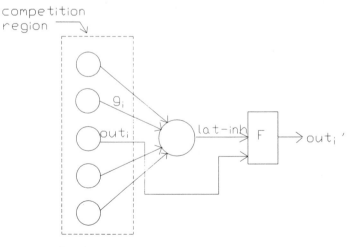

Figure 10-5. Improved Lateral Inhibition

The output of the inhibitory neuron OUT′ is then calculated as follows:

$$OUT' = [(1 + OUT_i)/(1 + LAT\_INHIB)] - 1$$

Because all of the calculations associated with this type of lateral inhibition are nonrecursive, they can be performed in one pass over the layer, thereby effecting a large reduction in computation.

This method of lateral inhibition solves another difficult problem. Suppose that a cell in layer 2 is firing vigorously, but the firing of adjacent cells decreases gradually with distance. Using conventional lateral inhibition, only the center cell will train; every other cell finds that there is at least one other cell in its competition region that has a higher output. With the new system of lateral inhibition, this situation cannot occur. A number of cells in a layer can be trained simultaneously, and training proceeds more reliably.

Receptive Region.   The analysis up to this point has been simplified by considering only one-dimensional layers. The cognitron is actually constructed of a cascade of two-dimensional layers, with a neuron in a given layer receiving inputs from a set of neurons on a portion of a two-dimensional plane comprising its connection region in the previous layer.

In this sense, the cognitron is organized much like the human visual cortex: a three-dimensional structure composed of several distinct two-dimensional layers. Each brain layer seems to represent different levels of generalization; that is, the input layer is sensitive to simple patterns, such as edges and their orientation in specific regions of the visual field, whereas the response of later layers is more complex, abstract, and position independent.

A similar function is achieved in the cognitron by emulating what is known of the cortical organization. Figure 10-6 shows that a cognitron neuron in layer 2 responds to a specific, small region of the input layer 1. A neuron in layer 3 connects to a set of layer 2 neurons, thereby responding indirectly to a larger set of layer 1 neurons. In a similar manner, neurons in subsequent layers are sensitive to larger areas of the input, until at the output layer, each neuron responds to the entire input field.

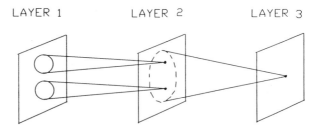

LAYER 1   LAYER 2   LAYER 3

Figure 10-6.   Cognitron Connection Regions

If the connection region of a neuron is of constant size in all layers, a large number of layers is required for the output layer neurons to cover the entire input field. The number of layers can be reduced if the connection region is increased in later layers. Unfortunately, this can result in so much overlap that the output layer neurons can show nearly identical responses. To solve this problem, cellular responses can be differentiated by increasing the size of the competition region. Because only one cell in a given competition region can fire, the effect of small differences in the response of cells is amplified.

Alternatively, the connections to a previous layer can be distributed probabilistically, with most synaptic connections being made in a limited region and with larger displacements occurring less often. This pattern mirrors the probabilistic distribution on neural synapses found in the brain. In the cognitron, it allows each output layer neuron to respond to the entire input field with only a modest number of layers.

Simulation Results.   Fukushima (1981) reports on a computer simulation of a four-layer cognitron intended to perform pattern recognition. Each layer consisted of a 12-by-12 array of excitatory neurons and an equal number of inhibitory neurons. The connection regions were square, covering 5-by-5 neurons. The competition regions were rhombic in shape, with both a height and a width of five neurons. Lateral inhibition covered a region of 7-by-7 neurons. The training rate parameters were set so that $q = 16.0$ and $q' = 2.0$. Synaptic weights were initialized at 0.

The network was trained by applying five stimulus patterns representing the arabic numerals 0 through 4 to the input layer. The network weights were adjusted after each numeral was applied, and the entire set was applied cyclically, until each pattern had been presented a total of 20 times.

The effectiveness of the training process was evaluated by running the network in reverse; that is, output patterns produced as responses from the network were applied to the output neurons and propagated back to the input layer. The patterns produced at the input layer could then be compared with the original input pattern. To do this, the normally unidirectional connections were assumed to conduct in the reverse direction, and lateral inhibition was disabled. Figure 10-7 shows typical test results. In column 2, the pattern produced by each numeral at the output was fed back, producing nearly perfect replicas of the original inputs. For column 4, only the neuron producing maximum output was applied to the output. The resulting patterns were as accurate as they were when the full output pattern was applied, except for the numeral 0, in which case the cell with maximal output was near the periphery and did not cover the entire input field.

THE NEOCOGNITRON

In an effort to improve the cognitron, Fukushima and his group have developed a powerful paradigm called the *neocognitron* (Fukushima 1984, 1986, 1987). While the two paradigms share certain similarities, they also show fundamental differences arising from the evolution of Fukushima's research. Both are multilayer hierarchical networks organized like the visual cortex. However, the neocognitron is more consistent with the visual-system model proposed by Hubel and Wiesel (1962, 1965, 1977). As a result, the neocognitron is far more powerful than the cognitron in its ability to recognize patterns despite translation, rotation, distortion, and changes in scale. Like the cognitron, the neocognitron generally uses self-organization for training, although a version has been described (Fukushima, Miyake, and Takayuki 1983) in which supervised learning was applied instead.

The neocognitron is oriented toward modeling the human visual system. As such, it accepts two-dimensional patterns like those

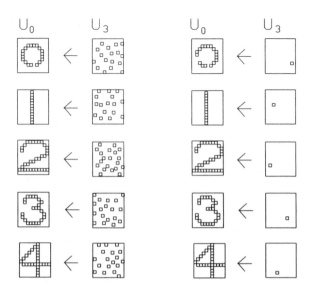

Figure 10-7. Cognitron Test Results

imaged onto the retina, and processes them in successive layers similar to those found in the human visual cortex. There is, of course, nothing in the neocognitron that limits it to processing visual data; it is quite versatile and may find widespread application as a general pattern-recognition paradigm.

In the visual cortex, cells have been found that respond to such features as lines and edges of specific orientations. In higher areas, cells respond to more complex and abstract figures, such as circles, triangles, and squares. At still higher levels, abstraction increases until cells can be identified that respond to faces and intricate shapes. Generally speaking, cells in the higher areas receive inputs from a group of lower-level cells. Hence, they respond to a wider area of the visual field. Responses of these high-level cells is less position dependent and more tolerant of distortion.

Structure

The neocognitron has a hierarchical structure intended to simulate the human visual system. As such, it consists of a succession of processing layers arranged in a hierarchical fashion (see Figure

10-8). An input pattern is applied to the first layer and passed through the planes comprising later layers until it arrives at the output layer, where the recognized pattern is indicated.

The structure of the neocognitron is difficult to diagram, but is conceptually simple. To emphasize its hierarchical nature (while simplifying the diagrams), a top-down analysis is used. That is, the neocognitron is shown to consist of layers. The layers are composed of sets of planes, and the planes are composed of cells.

Layers

Each layer of the neocognitron consists of two arrays of cell planes (see Figure 10-9). An array of simple-cell planes receives the outputs from the previous layer, detects specific patterns, and then passes them to an array of complex-cell planes, where they are processed to make the detected patterns less position dependent.

Planes

Within a layer, simple- and complex-cell planes exist as pairs; that is, for each simple-cell plane, there is a single complex-cell plane that processes its outputs. Each plane may be visualized as a two-dimensional array of cells.

Simple Cells

All cells in a given simple-cell plane respond to the same pattern. As shown in Figure 10-10, a simple-cell plane constitutes an array of cells, all of which are "tuned" to the same specific input pat-

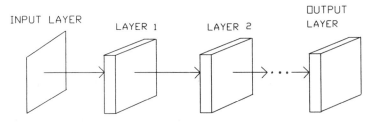

Figure 10-8. Neocognitron Layer Structure

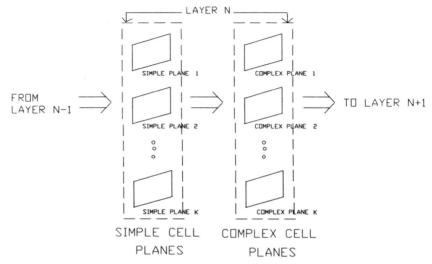

Figure 10-9. Neocognitron Plane Structure

tern. Each simple cell is sensitive to a restricted area of the input pattern, which is called its *receptive range*. For example, all cells in the top simple plane in Figure 10-10 respond to a C. If a C occurs in the input pattern to that layer, a cell responds if a "C" is detected in its receptive range.

Figure 10-10 shows that another plane of simple cells in that layer might respond to a 90° rotation of the C, another to a 180° rotation, and so on. If additional letters (and distorted versions thereof) are to be detected, an additional plane is required for each.

The receptive ranges of the cells in each simple plane overlap to cover the entire input pattern for that layer. Each cell receives inputs from corresponding regions of all complex planes in the previous layer. In this way, a simple cell responds to an occurrence of its tuned pattern in any complex plane of the previous layer, as long as it is within its receptive range.

Complex Cells

Complex cells serve to make the system less sensitive to the position of patterns in the input field. To accomplish this, each complex cell receives the outputs of a set of simple cells from its corresponding plane in the same layer. These simple cells cover a contiguous region of a simple plane, called the receptive range of the complex cell. The firing of any simple cell in this region is sufficient to cause the complex cell to fire. In this way, a complex cell responds to the same pattern as the simple cells in its corresponding plane, but it is less position sensitive than any one of them.

Thus, each layer of complex cells responds to a larger region of the input pattern than did those in the preceding layer. This progressive increase in range, from layer to layer, yields the desired decrease in the position sensitivity of the overall system.

Generalization

Each neuron in a layer near the input responds to a specific pattern in a precise location, such as an edge with a particular angular orientation at a given position. Each layer thereafter has a more abstract, less specific response, until at the output layer the complex cells respond to entire patterns, showing a high degree of insensitivity to their location, size, and orientation in the input

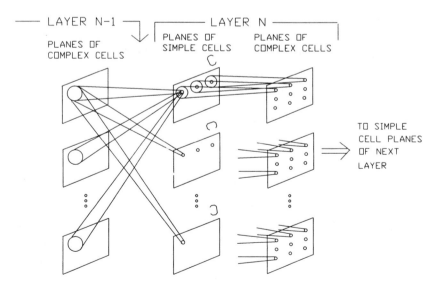

Figure 10-10. Neocognitron System

field. Used as a classifier, the output layer complex cell having the largest response indicates the detection of the associated pattern in the input field. Ideally, this detection is insensitive to the pattern's position, orientation, size, or other distortions.

Calculation

Simple cells in the neocognitron have exactly the same characteristics described above for the cognitron and use essentially the same formulas to determine their outputs. These are not repeated here.

The inhibitory cell produces an output that is proportional to the weighted-root mean square of its inputs. Note that the inputs to an inhibitory cell are identical to those of its associated simple cell and range over its responsive region in all complex planes. In symbols,

$$v = \sqrt{\left[\sum_i (b_i\, u_i)^2\right]}$$

where

v = the output of an inhibitory cell

i = ranges over all complex cells to which the inhibitory cell connects

b_i = the synaptic strength of the ith connection from a complex cell to the inhibitory cell

u_i = the output of the ith complex cell

The weights b_i are selected to decrease monotonically with distance from the center of the responsive region, and to have a sum of one.

Training

Only simple cells have adjustable weights. These connect to complex cells in the previous layer by means of modifiable synaptic strengths, adjusted during the training process to produce a maximal response to a specific stimulus feature. Some of these synapses are excitatory and tend to increase the cell's output, while others are inhibitory and reduce the output.

Figure 10-11 shows the complete arrangement of synapses between a simple cell and the complex cells in the preceding layer.

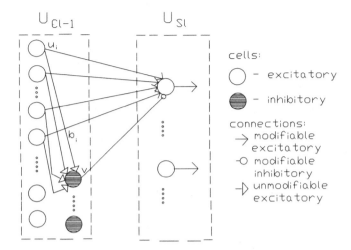

Figure 10-11. Connections from Complex Cells in One Layer to Simple Cells in the Next Layer

Each simple cell responds only to a set of complex cells within its receptive range. Also, an inhibitory cell exists that responds to exactly the same complex cells. Synaptic strengths of this inhibitory cell are not trained; they are selected so that the cell responds to the average of all cell outputs to which it connects. The single inhibitory synapse from the inhibitory cell to the simple cell is trained like any other synapse.

Unsupervised Training

To train the neocognitron, a pattern to be recognized is applied to the network input, and the synaptic strengths are adjusted layer by layer, starting with the set of simple cells nearest the input. The synaptic strength from each complex cell to a given simple cell is increased if, and only if, the two conditions that follow are satisfied: (1) the complex cell is responding; (2) the simple cell is responding more strongly than any of its immediate neighbors (within its competition area).

In this way, the simple cell is trained to respond most strongly to the patterns that occur most frequently in its receptive region, a characteristic that mirrors the development of pattern recognition found in experiments with cats. If no recognizable pattern is presented, the inhibitory cell serves to prevent random excitation.

The mathematics of training and the method for achieving lateral inhibition are similar to those described for the cognitron, so they are not repeated here. It should be noted that both simple- and complex-cell outputs are analog, continuous, and linear, and that the training algorithm ensures that they are nonnegative.

When a simple cell is selected to have its synaptic strengths increased, it serves as a representative for all cells in its plane, thereby causing their synaptic strengths to be increased in exactly the same pattern. In this way, all of the cells in a plane are trained to recognize the same feature and, after training, will do so regardless of its position in the field of complex cells in the preceding layer.

This system has a valuable self-repairing ability. If a given cell fails to function, another cell will be found to respond most strongly, and it will be trained to recognize the input pattern, thereby taking over the duties of its fallen comrade.

Supervised Training

In his earlier papers, Fukushima (Fukushima 1980; Fukushima and Miyake 1982) described the self-organizing, unsupervised training presented above. While this has produced impressive results, other experiments have been reported that use supervised training (Fukushima, Miyake, and Takayuki 1983). Here, the desired responses of each layer were chosen in advance by the experimenter. The weights were then adjusted using conventional two-layer training methods to produce the desired response. For example, the input layer was adjusted to recognize line segments in various orientations, much like the first layer of processing in the visual cortex. The layers that followed were trained to respond to successively more complex and abstract features, until at the output layer, the desired pattern was detected. While this effort produced a network that did an excellent job of recognizing handwritten Arabic numerals, the experimenters abandoned biological plausibility, seeking only to maximize the accuracy of the system result.

Training Implementation

In the usual configuration, the receptive field of each neuron is increased in each successive layer. Hence, the number of neurons per layer will decrease from input to output layers. Finally, the output layer has only one neuron per complex plane. Each such neuron represents a specific input pattern for which the network was trained. Used as a classifier, an input pattern is applied to the neocognitron and the outputs are calculated layer by layer, starting at the input layer. Because only a small section of the input pattern is observed by each simple cell in the input layer, typically, several simple cells sense features for which they have been trained and become active. In the next layer, more complex features are sensed as combinations of complex-cell outputs. Layer by layer, features are combined over an ever-increasing range; more complex features are detected, and position sensitivity is reduced.

Ideally, only a single neuron in the output layer should fire. Actually, several neurons will usually fire with varying strength and the input pattern must be determined from their relative outputs. If strong lateral inhibition is employed, only the neuron with the largest output will fire. However, taken by itself, this is often not the best answer. In practice, a simple function of a small group of the most vigorously firing neurons will often improve the accuracy of classification.

DISCUSSION

Both the cognitron and neocognitron are impressive in the accuracy with which they model the biological neural system. The fact that they produce results that mimic aspects of human learning and cognitive ability suggests that our understanding of the brain's function may be approaching a useful level.

The neocognitron is complex and requires substantial computational resources; hence, it seems unlikely that it is an optimal engineering solution for today's pattern-recognition problems. Since the 1960s, however, the cost of computation has been halved every two to three years, a pattern that will probably continue for at least another decade. Although approaches that were computationally infeasible a few years ago are common today and may seem trivial in a few more years, implementation of neocognitron models on a general-purpose computer is clearly inefficient. Thousandfold improvements in cost and performance need to be achieved by means of specialized architectures and custom VLSI (very large-scale integration) techniques to make the neocognitron a practical solution to complex pattern-recognition problems; however, neither this nor any other artificial neural network paradigm should be rejected solely on the basis of its computational requirements.

References

Blakemore, C., and Cooper, G. F. 1970. Development of the brain depends on the visual environment. *Nature* 228(5270):477–78.

Fukushima, K. 1975. Cognitron: A self-organizing multilayered neural network. *Biological Cybernetics* 20:121–36.

———. 1980. Neocognitron: A self-organizing neural network model for a mechanism of pattern recognition unaffected by shift in position. *Biological Cybernetics* 36(4):193–202.

———. 1981. Cognitron: A self-organizing multilayered neural network model. *NHK Technical Monograph*, No. 30, pp. 1–25. Available from Nippon Hoso Kyokai (Japanese Broadcasting Corp.), Technical Research Labs, Tokyo, Japan.

———. 1984. A hierarchical neural network model for associative memory. *Biological Cybernetics* 50:105–113.

———. 1986. A neural network model for selective attention in visual pattern recognition. *Biological Cybernetics* 55(1):5–15.

———. 1987. A neural network model for selective attention. In *Proceedings of the IEEE First International Conference on Neural Networks*, eds. M. Caudill and C. Butler, vol. 2, pp. 11–18. San Diego, CA: SOS Printing.

Fukushima, K., and Miyake, S. 1982. Neocognitron: A new algorithm for pattern recognition tolerant of deformations and shifts in position. *Pattern Recognition* 15(6):455–69.

Fukushima, K., Miyake, S., and Takayuki, I. 1983. Neocognitron: A neural network model for a mechanism of visual pattern recognition. *IEEE Transactions on Systems, Man and Cybernetics* SMC-13(5):826–34.

Hubel, D. H., and Wiesel, T. N. 1962. Receptive fields, binocular interaction and functional architecture in the cat's visual cortex. *Journal of Physiology* 160:106–54.

———. 1965. Receptive fields and functional architecture in two nonstriate visual areas (18 and 19) of the cat. *Journal of Neurophysiology* 28:229–89.

———. 1977. Functional architecture of macaque monkey visual cortex. *Proceedings of the Royal Society, London.* Ser. B 198, pp. 1–59.

Appendix A

The Biological Neural Network

THE HUMAN BRAIN: A BIOLOGICAL MODEL FOR ARTIFICIAL NEURAL NETWORKS

The structure of artificial neural networks has been modeled after the organization of the human brain. As we point out, this similarity is actually slight, yet even this modest emulation of the brain has yielded impressive results. For example, artificial neural networks exhibit such brainlike characteristics as their ability to learn from experience, generalize on their knowledge, perform abstraction, and make errors, all more characteristic of human thought than of human-made computers.

With the successes achieved using a crude approximation of the brain, it would seem reasonable to expect further advances from a more accurate model. Developing such a model requires a detailed understanding of the structure and function of the brain. This, in turn, demands a complete characterization of the neurons that comprise its computational and communication elements. Unfortunately, this information is by no means complete; much of the brain remains shrouded in mystery. Major pathways have been laid out and certain areas identified by function, but nothing approaching a complete "schematic" exists. The biochemistry of the neuron, the brain's fundamental building block, continues to yield its secrets reluctantly. Each year brings new information regarding the neuron's electrochemical behavior, always in the direction of exposing new levels of complexity. One thing is certain: the neuron is far more intricate than was suspected a few years ago, and no one claims to have a full understanding of its operation.

Despite our limited knowledge, enough is known to make the brain a model worth studying in our quest for better artificial neural networks. Through eons of trial and error, evolution has probably arrived at a structure optimally suited to solving the problems that commonly confront the human organism. It seems unlikely that we will invent a better solution. By carefully emulating the brain, we are availing ourselves of nature's research (at no cost) and will probably reproduce more of the brain's abilities.

This appendix contains the barest outline of the current knowledge regarding the structure and function of the brain. Although it is much abbreviated, every effort has been made to preserve accuracy. The sections that follow should serve to illuminate the information in the text of this volume and I hope will stimulate interest in the biological system and generate ideas that lead to better artificial neural networks.

ORGANIZATION OF THE HUMAN BRAIN

A human brain contains over one hundred billion computing elements called *neurons*. Exceeding the stars in our Milky Way galaxy in number, these neurons communicate throughout the body by way of nerve fibers that make perhaps one hundred trillion connections called *synapses*. This network of neurons is responsible for all of the phenomena that we call thought, emotion, and cognition, as well as for performing myriad sensorimotor and autonomic functions. The exact manner in which this is accomplished is little understood, but much of the physiological structure has been mapped, and certain functional areas are gradually yielding to determined research.

The brain also contains a dense network of blood vessels that provide oxygen and nutrients to the neurons and other tissues. This blood supply is connected to the main circulatory system by a highly effective filtration system called the *blood–brain barrier*, a protective mechanism that isolates the brain from potentially toxic substances found in the bloodstream. Isolation is maintained by the low permeability of the brain's blood vessels, and also by the tight coverings of glial cells that surround the neurons. In addition to their other functions, these glial cells provide the structural scaffolding for the brain. Virtually all of the brain's volume not occupied by neurons and blood vessels is filled with glial cells.

The blood–brain barrier is essential to the safety of the brain, but it greatly complicates the administration of therapeutic drugs. It also frustrates researchers, who would like to observe the effects of a wide variety of chemicals on the brain's function. Only a short list of drugs designed to affect the brain will cross this barrier. These drugs consist of small molecules capable of slipping through the tiny pores in the blood vessels. To affect brain function, they must then pass through the glial cell or be soluble in its membrane. Few molecules of interest satisfy these requirements; molecules of many therapeutic drugs are stopped by this barrier.

The brain is the most concentrated consumer of energy in the body. Comprising only 2% of body mass, at rest it uses over 20% of the body's oxygen. Even while we sleep, the energy consumption continues unabated. In fact, there is evidence that it may actually increase during REM-sleep periods. Consuming only 20 watts, the brain is an incredibly energy efficient organ. Computers, with only a tiny fraction of the brain's computational ability, consume many thousands of watts and require elaborate provisions for cooling to prevent their thermal self-destruction.

The Neuron

The neuron is the fundamental building block of the nervous system. It is a cell similar to all cells in the body; however, certain critical specializations allow it to perform all of the computational and communication functions within the brain.

As shown in Figure A-1, the neuron consists of three sections: the cell body, the dendrites, and the axon, each with separate but complementary functions.

Functionally, the dendrites receive the signals from other cells at connection points called synapses. From there, the signals are passed on to the cell body where they are essentially averaged with other such signals. If the average over a short time interval is suffi-

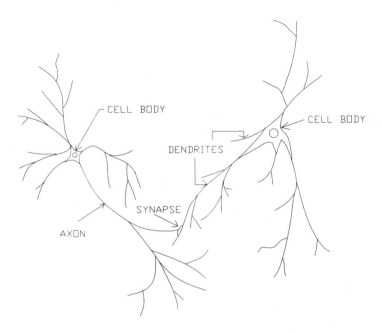

Figure A-1. Components of a Neuron

ciently large, the cell "fires," producing a pulse down its axon that is passed on to succeeding cells. Despite its apparent simplicity, this computational function accounts for most of the known activity of the brain. Underlying it, however, is a complex electrochemical system. We examine the functions of that system in the sections that follow.

The Cell Body

The neurons in the adult brain do not regenerate; they must last a lifetime. This means that all of the components must be continuously replaced and the materials renewed as needed. Most of these maintenance activities take place in the cell body, where a veritable chemical factory manufactures a wide variety of complex molecules. In addition, the cell body manages the energy economy of the neuron and regulates a host of other activities within the cell.

The outer membrane of the neuron's cell body has the unique capability of generating nerve impulses, a vital function of the nervous system and central to its computational abilities.

Hundreds of neuron types have been identified, each with a distinctively shaped cell body (see Figure A-2), which is usually 5 to 100 microns in diameter. Once thought to be mere random variations, these differing morphological configurations are being found to exhibit important functional specializations. Identification of the functions of the various cell types is currently a topic of intensive research and is essential to an understanding of the processing mechanisms within the brain.

Dendrites

Most input signals from other neurons enter the cell by way of the dendrites, a bushy branching structure emanating from the cell body. On the dendrites are synaptic connections where signals are

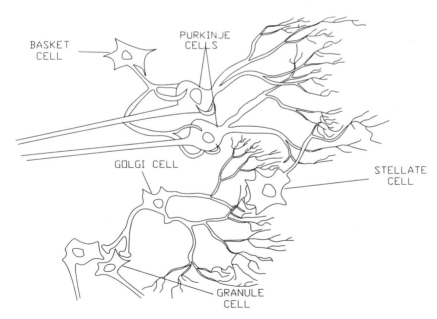

Figure A-2.   Types of Neurons

received, usually from other axons. In addition, there are a significant number of synaptic connections from axon to axon, axon to cell body, and dendrite to dendrite; the function of these is little understood, but too widespread to be insignificant.

Unlike electrical circuits, there is usually no physical or electrical connection made at the synapse. Instead, a narrow gap called the *synaptic cleft* separates the dendrite from the transmitting axon. Specialized chemicals that are released by the axon into the synaptic cleft diffuse across to the dendrite. These chemicals, called *neurotransmitters*, pass into specific receptor sites on the dendrite and enter the cell body.

More than thirty neurotransmitters have been identified. Some are excitatory and tend to cause the cell to "fire" and produce an output pulse. Others are inhibitory and tend to suppress such a pulse. The cell body combines the signals received over its dendrites and, if their resultant signal is above its threshold, a pulse is produced that propagates down the axon to other neurons.

The Axon

An axon may be as short as 0.1 millimeter, or it can exceed 1 meter in length, extending to an entirely different part of the body. Near its end, the axon has multiple branches, each terminating in a synapse, where the signal is transmitted to the another neuron through a dendrite or, in some cases, directly to a cell body. In this way, a single neuron can generate a pulse that will activate or inhibit hundreds or thousands of other neurons, each of which can in turn (through its dendrites) be acted upon by hundreds or thousands of other neurons. Thus, it is this high degree of connectivity rather than the functional complexity of the neuron itself that gives the neuron its computational power.

The synaptic connection that terminates a branch of the axon is a small, bulbous expansion containing spherical structures called *synaptic vesicles*, each of which contains a great number of neurotransmitter molecules. When a nerve impulse arrives down the axon, some of these vesicles release their contents into the synaptic cleft, thereby initiating the process of interneuron communication (see Figure A-3).

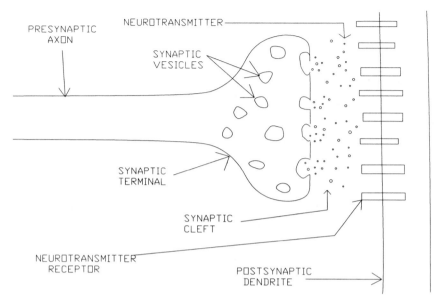

Figure A-3.   Synapse

In addition to the all-or-nothing behavior just discussed, weakly stimulated neurons also transmit electrochemical signals through their interior with a graded response. Local in nature, these signals die out rapidly with distance unless reinforced. Nature makes use of this cellular characteristic in the peripheral nervous system by wrapping axons in Schwann cells, thereby forming an insulating sheath known as myelin. This myelin sheath is interrupted every millimeter or so along the axon at narrow gaps called the *nodes of Ranvier*. Nerve impulses passing down an axon jump from node to node, propagating by a graded response mode in between. In this way, the axon need not expend energy to maintain its chemical gradients along its entire length. Only at the exposed nodes is the action potential regenerated; more efficient graded responses suffice for intermediate transmission. In addition to saving energy, other functions of this sheath have been discovered. For example, myelinated nerve fibers transmit signals more rapidly. Several diseases have been traced to the deterioration of this insulation, and it is suspected as a contributor to others.

The Cellular Membrane

Communication in the brain is of two types: chemical signals across the synapses, and electrical signals within the neuron. It is the wonderfully complex action of the membrane that creates the cell's ability to produce and transmit both kinds of signals.

The cellular membrane is about five nanometers thick and consists of two layers of lipid molecules. Embedded in the membrane are various specific proteins that fall into five classes: pumps, channels, receptors, enzymes, and structural proteins.

Pumps actively move ions across the cell's membrane to maintain concentration gradients. Channels pass ions selectively and control their flow through the membrane. Some channels are opened or closed by the prevailing electrical potential across the membrane, thereby providing a rapid and sensitive means of modulating ionic gradients. Other types of channels are chemically controlled, changing their permeability upon receipt of chemical messengers.

Receptors are proteins that recognize and attach many types of molecules in the cellular environment with great specificity. Enzymes in or near the membrane speed a variety of chemical reactions. Structural proteins interconnect cells and help to maintain the structure of the cell itself.

The cell's internal sodium concentration is ten times lower than its surroundings and its potassium concentration is ten times higher. These concentrations tend to equalize through leaks in the cell due to pores in the membrane. To maintain the necessary concentrations, a membrane protein, called a sodium pump, continuously passes sodium out of the cell and potassium into the cell. Each pump moves roughly two hundred sodium atoms and one hundred thirty potassium ions per second. A neuron may have millions of such pumps, moving hundreds of millions of ions in and out of the cell each second. The potassium concentration within the cell is further increased by the presence of a large number of permanently open potassium channels; that is, there are proteins that pass potassium ions readily into the cell, but inhibit the passage of sodium. The combination of these two mechanisms is responsible for creating and maintaining the dynamic chemical equilibrium that constitutes the resting state of the neuron.

The ionic concentration gradient across the cell membrane

causes the interior of the cell to assume an electrical potential of
− 70 millivolts relative to its surroundings. For the cell to fire
(producing an action potential), the synaptic inputs must reduce
this level to approximately − 50 millivolts. When this occurs, sodium and potassium flows are suddenly reversed; within a milli-
second the interior of the cell becomes 50 millivolts positive relative to external environment. This polarity reversal spreads rapidly
through the cell, causing the nerve impulse to propagate down the
length of the axon to its presynaptic connections. When the impulse arrives at the terminal of an axon, voltage-controlled calcium
channels are opened. This triggers the release of neurotransmitter
molecules into the synaptic cleft and the process continues on to
other neurons. After generating an action potential, the cell enters
a refractory period of several milliseconds, during which it returns
to its resting potential in preparation for the generation of another
pulse.

Examining this process in greater detail, the initial receipt of
neurotransmitter molecules lowers the internal potential of the cell
from − 70 millivolts to − 50 millivolts. At this point, voltage-controlled sodium channels are opened, allowing sodium to flood into
the cell. This further reduces the potential, increases the sodium
flow, and creates a self-reinforcing process that quickly propagates
to adjacent regions, reversing the local-cell potential from negative
to positive as it goes.

Shortly after opening, the sodium channels close and potassium
channels open. This allows potassium to flow out of the cell, and
the − 70 millivolt internal potential is restored. This rapid voltage
reversal constitutes the action potential, which propagates rapidly
along the full length of the axon like a row of tumbling dominoes.

The sodium and potassium channels respond to cell potentials;
hence, they are said to be voltage gated. Another type of channel is
chemically gated. It opens only when a specific neurotransmitter
molecule binds to a receptor, and it is quite insensitive to voltage.
Such channels are found in the postsynaptic connections on the
dendrites and are responsible for the neuron's response to the
various neurotransmitter molecules. The acetylcholine protein
that combines with a receptor is one such chemically gated channel. When a packet of acetylcholine molecules is released into the
synaptic cleft, it diffuses to acetylcholine receptors embedded in
the postsynaptic membrane. These receptors (which are also chan-

nels) then open, allowing free passage of both potassium and sodium across the membrane. This produces a brief local reduction in the negative internal potential of the cell (constituting a positive pulse). Because they are short and small, many such channel openings are required to cause the cell to produce an action potential, although each produces a graded response.

Acetylcholine receptors/channels pass both sodium and potassium, thereby producing positive pulses. Such pulses are excitatory, as they contribute to the production of an action potential. Other chemically gated channels pass only potassium ions out of the cell, and produce negative pulses; these are inhibitory, as they tend to prevent the cell from firing.

Gamma-aminobutyric acid (GABA) is one of the most common inhibitory neurotransmitters. Found almost exclusively in the brain and spinal cord, it binds to a receptor with a channel that selectively passes chloride ions. Upon entry, these ions increase the negative potential of the cell, and thereby inhibit firing. GABA deficiency has been associated with Huntington's chorea, an inherited neurological syndrome causing uncontrolled muscular motions. Unfortunately, the blood-brain barrier has so far prevented augmentation of the GABA supply, and no other treatment has been discovered. It seems probable that other neurological disorders and mental illnesses will be traced to similar defects in the neurotransmitters or their chemical precursors.

The firing rate of a neuron is determined by the cumulative effect of a large number of excitatory and inhibitory inputs, roughly averaged by the cell body over a short time interval. Receipt of excitatory neurotransmitter molecules will increase the firing rate of a neuron; a smaller number, or a mixture with inhibitory inputs will reduce the firing rate. In this way, the neuron signal is pulse-rate or frequency modulated (FM). This modulation method, widely used in communication engineering (FM radio is an example), has proven to have significant advantages in noise rejection over other techniques.

Research has disclosed a bewildering biochemical complexity in the brain. For example, over thirty substances are thought to be neurotransmitters, and there are a large number of receptors with various response modes. Furthermore, the action of a particular neurotransmitter molecule depends upon the type of receptor in the postsynaptic membrane; the same neurotransmitter may be excitatory at one synapse and inhibitory at another. Also, a "second messenger" system is at work in the cell, where receipt of a neurotransmitter triggers the production of large numbers of cyclic adenosine triphosphate molecules, thereby producing a greatly amplified physiological response.

Researchers always hope to find a simple pattern that unifies complex and diverse observations. So far, this has not been the case with neurobiological studies. Most discoveries have exposed more ignorance than they have eliminated. One such result of neural research has been a rapid proliferation in the number and types of electrochemical activities recognized to be at work in the brain; the task remains to combine them into a coherent functional model.

COMPUTERS AND THE HUMAN BRAIN

There are similarities between the brain and the digital computer: both operate on electrical signals; both are a composition of a large number of simple elements; and both perform functions that are, broadly speaking, computational. There are, however, fundamental differences. Compared to the microsecond or even nanosecond time scales of modern digital computation, nerve impulses are astoundingly slow. With each neuron requiring milliseconds between signal transmissions, the brain's huge computation rate is achieved by a tremendous number of parallel computational units, far beyond any proposed for a computer system. Error rates represent another fundamental difference; the electronic digital computer is inherently error free, so long as its input is perfectly correct and its hardware and software are intact. The brain often produces best guesses and approximations from partially incomplete and incorrect inputs. Frequently, it is wrong. But its error rate has been adequate to ensure our survival for millions of years.

The first digital computers were often referred to as "electronic brains." Viewed in the light of our current knowledge about the complexity of the brain, this was optimistic to say the least. In any case, the appellation is simply inappropriate. The two systems differ in every particular. They are optimized to solve different types of problems, have fundamentally different structures, and are evaluated by different criteria.

Some say artificial neural networks will someday duplicate the function of the human brain. Before this is even thinkable, the brain's organization and function must be understood, a task that probably will not be achieved in the near future. This volume points out that current artificial neural networks are based upon a highly simplified model that ignores most of what is known about the detailed functioning of the brain. It seems reasonable to expect that a more accurate model would produce a closer emulation of the brain's operation.

Breakthroughs in artificial neural networks will require the strengthening of their theoretical foundations. Theoretical advances, in turn, must be preceded by improved mathematical methods, as research is seriously hampered by our inability to deal with these systems in a quantitative manner. This fact is sobering when one considers that the current limited level of mathematical support has been achieved with monumental effort by some of the world's most brilliant researchers. In fact, the analytical problem is extraordinarily difficult, involving as it does highly complex, nonlinear, dynamical systems. It may be that entirely new mathematical methods must be developed to cope with a system having the complexity of the human brain; or perhaps no fully satisfactory mathematics can ever be devised.

In spite of the problems, efforts to model the human brain continue to produce fascinating, tantalizing results that inspire further effort. Successful models, based upon speculations about the brain's structure, lead neuroanatomists and neurophysiologists to reexamine their observations, looking for corresponding structures and functions. Conversely, advances in the biological sciences have led to modified and elaborated artificial models. Simultaneously, engineers are applying the artificial models to real-world problems and are producing encouraging results, despite the lack of a full understanding.

The convergence of disciplines onto the problem of artificial neural networks has brought a richness of inquiry that may be unprecedented in the history of science. Biologists, anatomists, physiologists, engineers, mathematicians, and even philosophers are actively involved in the study. The problems are staggering, but the goal is lofty: an understanding of human thought itself.

Appendix B

Vector and Matrix Operations

INTRODUCTION

Linear algebra comprises a large body of knowledge about vectors and matrixes. This appendix presents only a small portion of the notation and a few of the manipulations used in this field. Despite the fragmentary nature of the treatment, it will prove highly useful in the study of artificial neural networks. Vector notation reduces complicated expressions to a few symbols, thereby clarifying the principles and easing comprehension. Vector operations manipulate entire groups of data with a single symbol; thus, larger conceptual "chunks" can be handled without concern for the details. Finally, vectors have geometric significance, a fact that permits visualization of the concepts.

The sections that follow are intended for those who have never studied linear algebra, and those who feel the need for a review before launching into this volume. Little theory is presented; there are many excellent texts on the subject, such as the one by Anton (1977). Also, there is a highly accessible introductory treatment by Jordan (1986) that is specifically intended for artificial neural network studies.

VECTORS

Artificial neural network computations involve the manipulation of ordered sets of numbers. An ordered set is simply a group of numbers in a specific order; that is, there is a first number, a second number, and so on. Such ordered sets are called *vectors*. While it is possible to consider each element of a set separately, giving each a name, it is much simpler if we name the entire set. For example, suppose we are considering the ordered set of numbers 6, 7, 4. We could refer to the set of numbers as "the ordered set of three numbers where the first number is 6, the second number is 7, and the third number is 4." However, this is verbose and takes time to decipher. A more compact method designates the elements of the vector as $i1$, $i2$, and $i3$ where $i_1 = 6$, $i_2 = 7$, and $i_3 = 4$. The vector is then written ($i1$, $i2$, $i3$). Still more compactly, the entire set can be given the name **I** (traditionally written in uppercase boldface letters.) Once we have defined the number of elements, vectors of any size can be referred to by a single letter!

Vector Addition

The benefits of vector notation go much further when we wish to perform operations on vectors. For example, if we wish to add two vectors **I** and **J**, element by element, we can indicate this operation as **I** + **J**. In expanded notation, this would be written as

$$\mathbf{I} + \mathbf{J} = (i_1 + j_1, \ i_2 + j_2, \ i_3 + j_3, \ \ldots, \ i_n + j_n)$$

It may be seen that the sum of two vectors is another vector.

As an example of addition, assume the two vectors **I** and **J** have the values that follow:

$$\mathbf{I} = (3, 4, 2)$$

$$\mathbf{J} = (2, 3, 1)$$

Then their sum can be written

$$\mathbf{I} + \mathbf{J} = (5, 7, 3)$$

Dot Product

A second common operation is the *dot product* of two vectors (sometimes called the inner product). Here, the vectors are simply lined up, their corresponding components are multiplied together, and all of the resulting products are summed. This operation takes two vectors and produces a single number (a scalar). For example,

$$\mathbf{I} \cdot \mathbf{J} \text{ (pronounced ``I dot J'')} = (i_1 \times j_1) + (i_2 \times j_2) + \ldots + (i_n \times j_n)$$

If, for example,

$$\mathbf{I} = (3, 4, 2)$$

$$\mathbf{J} = (2, 3, 1)$$

then $\mathbf{I} \cdot \mathbf{J} = (3 \times 2) + (4 \times 3) + (2 \times 1) = 6 + 12 + 2 = 20$.

Note that the dot product operation can be performed only on vectors having the same number of elements.

Vectors as Line Segments

In addition to simplifying notation, vectors have geometric interpretations that can help to visualize certain problems. For example, a vector with two elements can be considered to represent a point (a, b) on the x–y plane (see Figure B-1). The first element of the vector represents the distance between that point and the y axis, while the second element represents its distance from the x axis. Alternatively, a vector can be viewed as a line segment joining the origin to this point. Both interpretations are useful under different circumstances.

Similarly, a vector with three components can represent a line

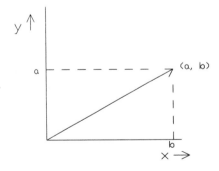

Figure B-1.   Vector as a Point of the x–y Plane

segment in three-dimensional space; vectors with more components may be thought of as line segments in higher-dimensional "hyperspace." It is difficult to visualize spaces of more than three dimensions, but many important concepts can be expressed in the familiar three-dimensional space and extended by generalization into higher dimensions. Conversely, a vexing problem in a high-dimensional space can often be considered in one, two, or three dimensions and a geometric understanding can be achieved.

Row and Column Vectors

Sometimes a vector is written as a horizontal sequence of numbers, such as (4, 5, 9). In this case, it is called a row vector. For other purposes, a vector may be written vertically as

$$\begin{bmatrix} 4 \\ 5 \\ 9 \end{bmatrix}$$

and would be called a column vector. Unless otherwise stated, all vectors in this volume are row vectors.

Vector Transposition

The vector transposition operation converts a row vector to a column vector, or vice versa. The column vector version of a row vector is written $\mathbf{V}^t$, and is read "V transpose."

If, for example,

$$\mathbf{V} = (2, 4, 3)$$

then

$$\mathbf{V}^t = \begin{bmatrix} 2 \\ 4 \\ 3 \end{bmatrix}$$

MATRIXES

A matrix is a rectangular array of numbers, such as

$$\begin{bmatrix} 3 & 6 & 9 \\ 4 & 2 & 8 \\ 5 & 4 & 1 \end{bmatrix}$$

It is customary to refer to this set of numbers using a boldface uppercase character, such as **M**. The elements of a matrix are referenced by the same character in lowercase, followed by a subscript. For example, the element in the second row and third column would be referenced as $m_{2,3}$.

Matrix Addition

Two matrixes are added just like two vectors, component by component. For example,

$$\text{if } \mathbf{M} = \begin{bmatrix} 3 & 2 & 1 \\ 4 & 1 & 3 \\ 1 & 3 & 5 \end{bmatrix} \quad \text{and } \mathbf{N} = \begin{bmatrix} 2 & 2 & 1 \\ 3 & 1 & 2 \\ 4 & 2 & 1 \end{bmatrix}$$

$$\text{then } \mathbf{M} + \mathbf{N} = \begin{bmatrix} 5 & 4 & 2 \\ 7 & 2 & 5 \\ 5 & 5 & 6 \end{bmatrix}$$

Multiplying a Matrix by a Vector

Multiplying a matrix by a vector is performed frequently in artificial neural network calculations. It is done by treating each column of the matrix as a vector and finding its dot product with the multiplier vector. The resulting numbers form a new vector, with the dot product with column 1 producing the first component, the dot product with column 2 producing the second, and so on. For example, if we have a matrix **M** to be multiplied by a vector **X**, it would be done as follows:

$$(2 \quad 4 \quad 6) \begin{bmatrix} 3 & 4 & 1 \\ 2 & 3 & 5 \\ 1 & 2 & 1 \end{bmatrix}$$

First, find the dot product of the vector **X** with the first column vector of the matrix **M**. This becomes the first component of the product vector **P**.

$$p_1 = (2 \times 3) + (4 \times 2) + (6 \times 1) = 20$$

Similarly,

$$p_2 = (2 \times 4) + (4 \times 3) + (6 \times 2) = 32$$
$$p_3 = (2 \times 1) + (4 \times 5) + (6 \times 1) = 28$$

Thus, **P** = (20, 32, 28). Cautions:

1. Matrix multiplication is not commutative. **X M** is not equal to **M X**.
2. The number of components in the vector must equal the number of rows in the matrix.

Matrix Multiplication

Two matrixes may be multiplied by a method that is an extension of the method described for multiplying a vector by a matrix. To perform this operation, find all possible dot products involving the row vectors of the multiplier matrix (on the left), with the column vectors of the multiplicand matrix (on the right). Each dot product becomes an element of the product matrix, which has as many rows as the multiplier and as many columns as the multiplicand. The position of each product in the product matrix is determined by the row and column used to produce it. For example, if a dot product was formed by multiplying row 2 of the multiplier matrix by column 3 of the multiplicand matrix, the dot product would go into row 2, column 3 of the product matrix. If, for example,

$$M = \begin{bmatrix} 1 & 3 & 2 \\ 2 & 3 & 5 \\ 3 & 1 & 4 \end{bmatrix}$$

and

$$N = \begin{bmatrix} 3 & 3 & 1 \\ 4 & 2 & 1 \\ 3 & 1 & 2 \end{bmatrix}$$

then, to find the product matrix **P** where

$$P = M\,N$$

first find the dot product of the first row vector of **M** with the first column vector of **N**

$$(1 \quad 3 \quad 2) \cdot \begin{bmatrix} 3 \\ 4 \\ 3 \end{bmatrix} = (1 \times 3) + (3 \times 4) + (2 \times 3) = 3 + 12 + 6 = 21$$

The element p_{11} is, therefore, 21.

This matrix multiplication will require calculating nine dot products, one for each position in the product array. The product will be as follows:

$$P = \begin{bmatrix} 21 & 11 & 8 \\ 33 & 17 & 15 \\ 25 & 15 & 12 \end{bmatrix}$$

Two matrixes can be multiplied only if the number of columns in the multiplier—the matrix on the left—equals the number of rows of the multiplicand. The resulting product matrix will have the same number of rows as the multiplier, and the same number of columns as the multiplicand.

Matrix Transposition

Just as a vector transposition changes a row vector into a column vector, a matrix transposition changes all row vectors into column vectors. To do so, simply make each row vector a column vector in the transpose. Row 1 becomes column 1, row 2 becomes column 2, and so on. The left-most element in a row becomes the top element in the column. An easy way to remember the operation is that the subscripts of each element are interchanged; that is,

$$m_{3,2} \text{ becomes } m_{2,3}$$

For example, if

$$\mathbf{M} = \begin{bmatrix} 3 & 2 & 1 \\ 4 & 1 & 5 \\ 2 & 1 & 3 \end{bmatrix}$$

then

$$\mathbf{M}' = \begin{bmatrix} 3 & 4 & 2 \\ 2 & 1 & 1 \\ 1 & 5 & 3 \end{bmatrix}$$

Matrixes as Vectors

A row vector can be seen to be a special case of a matrix, that is, a matrix having a single row. Similarly, the dot product operation may be considered as a matrix multiplication in which there is only one row in the multiplier and one column in the multiplicand.

For these reasons, mathematicians will often treat vectors as special cases of matrixes; both are designated by upper-case boldface letters and may be mixed in expressions.

Outer Products

The outer-product operation treats row and column vectors as matrixes. It computes the product of a column vector and a row vector and produces a matrix as a result. This is an ordinary matrix multiplication, using the standard computational procedure previously described.

For example, suppose that we wish to multiply the row vector **R** by the column vector **C**, where

$$\mathbf{R} = (1, \ 3, \ 2)$$
$$\mathbf{C} = \begin{bmatrix} 2 \\ 4 \\ 1 \end{bmatrix}$$

then

$$\mathbf{P} = \mathbf{C} \, \mathbf{R} = \begin{bmatrix} 2 \\ 4 \\ 1 \end{bmatrix} [1 \ \ 3 \ \ 2]$$

To find the element $\mathbf{P}_{2,3}$, multiply the element in row 2 of **C** by the element in column 3 of **R**; hence, $\mathbf{P}_{2,3} = 4 \times 2 = 8$. In general, $\mathbf{P}_{ij} = \mathbf{C}_i \times \mathbf{R}_j$, and the full outer product is written

$$\mathbf{P} = \begin{bmatrix} 2 & 6 & 4 \\ 4 & 12 & 8 \\ 1 & 3 & 2 \end{bmatrix}$$

Special Operations

There is no standard operator for multiplying two vectors together component by component, as is done for addition. Because this is an operation frequently required for artificial neural networks, a special operator $ has been defined for use in this volume. If, therefore,

$$\mathbf{P} = (1, 3, 2) \text{ and } \mathbf{Q} = (2, 1, 4)$$

then

$$\mathbf{P} \ \$ \ \mathbf{Q} = (1 \times 2, 3 \times 1, 2 \times 4) = (2, 3, 8)$$

It is important to distinguish between this operation and the dot product. Both accept two vectors as operands; the dot product produces a single number (a scalar), whereas the $ operator produces another vector of the same size.

References

Anton, H. 1977. *Elementary linear algebra*. New York: Wiley.

Jordan, M. I. 1986. An introduction to linear algebra in parallel distributed processing. In *Parallel distributed processing*, vol. 1, pp. 365–422. Cambridge, MA: MIT Press.

Appendix C

Training Algorithms

Artificial neural networks have been trained by a wide variety of methods. Fortunately, most training techniques have been developed from common roots and share many characteristics. The purpose of this appendix is to present a review of certain fundamental algorithms, in terms of both their current applicability and their historical significance. Given this perspective, other related algorithms will be more easily understood and new developments can be better comprehended and evaluated.

SUPERVISED AND UNSUPERVISED LEARNING

Training algorithms may be classified as supervised or unsupervised. In supervised training, there is a teacher that presents input patterns to the network, compares the resulting outputs with those desired, and then adjusts the network weights in such a way as to reduce the difference. It is difficult to conceive of such a teaching mechanism in biological systems; hence, while this approach has enjoyed much success in applications, it is disdained by those who believe that artificial neural networks must ultimately use the same mechanisms as the human brain.

Unsupervised training requires no teacher; input patterns are applied, and the network self-organizes by adjusting its weights according to a well-defined algorithm. Because no desired output is specified during the training process, the results are unpredictable in terms of firing patterns of specific neurons. What does occur, however, is that the network organizes in a fashion that develops emergent properties of the training set. For example, input patterns may be classified according to their degree of similarity, with similar patterns activating the same output neuron.

HEBBIAN LEARNING

The work of D. O. Hebb (1949) has provided the inspiration for most of the training algorithms that have been subsequently developed. Prior to Hebb's work, it was generally recognized that learning in a biological system involved some physical change to the neurons, but no one had a clear idea how this might actually take place.

Based upon physiological and psychological research, Hebb presented an intuitively appealing hypothesis about how a set of biological neurons might learn. His theory involved only local interactions between neurons with no global teacher; hence, the training is unsupervised. While his work did not include a mathematical analysis, his ideas were so clear and compelling that they received nearly universal acceptance. His book became a classic that is still widely studied by those with a serious interest in the field.

Hebbian Learning Algorithm

In essence, Hebb proposed that a synapse connecting two neurons is strengthened whenever both of those neurons fire. This may be thought of as strengthening a synapse according to the correlation between the excitation levels of the neurons that it connects. For that reason Hebbian learning is sometimes called correlation learning.

This idea is expressed in the equation that follows:

$$w_{ij}(t + 1) = w_{ij}(t) + \text{NET}_i \, \text{NET}_j$$

where

$w_{ij}(t)$ = the synaptic strength from neuron i to neuron j at time t
NET_i = the excitation level of the source neuron
NET_j = the excitation level of the destination neuron

Hebb's concept answered the perplexing question of how learning could take place without a teacher. In the Hebbian system, learning is a purely local phenomenon, involving only two neurons and a synapse; no global feedback system is required for the neural patterns to develop.

Subsequent work with Hebbian learning produced many successes, but also disclosed its limitations; some patterns simply could not be learned by this method. As a result there have been numerous extensions and innovations, most of which owe a heavy debt to the work of Hebb.

Signal Hebbian Learning

As we have seen, the NET output of a simple artificial neuron is the weighted sum of its inputs. This may be expressed as follows:

$$NET_j = \sum_i OUT_i w_{ij}$$

where
   NET_j = the net output of neuron j
   OUT_i = the output of neuron i
    w_{ij} = the weight connecting neuron i to neuron j

It can be shown that linear multilayer networks are no more powerful than a single-layer network; the representational ability of the network can be improved only by introducing a nonlinearity into the transfer function of the neuron. A network using the sigmoidal activation function with Hebbian learning is said to employ signal Hebbian learning. In this case, the Hebbian equations are modified to the form that follows:

$$OUT_i = 1/[1 + e^{-NET_i}] = F(NET_i)$$

$$w_{ij}(t + 1) = w_{ij}(t) + OUT_i\, OUT_j$$

where
   $w_{ij}(t)$ = the synaptic strength from neuron i to neuron j at time t
   OUT_i = the output level of the source neuron = $F(NET_i)$

OUT_j = the output level of the destination neuron = $F(NET_j)$

Differential Hebbian Learning

A variant of signal Hebbian learning calculates the product of the previous changes of the outputs to determine the weight change. This method, called differential Hebbian learning, uses the equations that follow:

$$w_{ij}(t + 1) = w_{ij}(t) + [OUT_i(t) - OUT_i(t - 1)][OUT_j(t) - OUT_j(t - 1)]$$

where

$w_{ij}(t)$ = the synaptic strength from neuron i to neuron j at time t

$OUT_i(t)$ = the output level of the source neuron at time t

$OUT_j(t)$ = the output level of the destination neuron at time t

INSTARS AND OUTSTARS

Many of the ideas commonly used in artificial neural networks can be traced to the work of Stephen Grossberg; so it is with the instar and outstar configurations (Grossberg 1974) that have found their way into many network paradigms. An instar, as shown in Figure C-1, consists of a neuron fed by a set of inputs through synaptic weights. An outstar, shown in Figure C-2, is a neuron driving a set of weights. Instars and outstars can be interconnected to form arbitrarily complex networks, and Grossberg proposed them as a model for certain biological functions. Their starlike appearance suggests their name; however, they are not usually diagrammed this way in networks.

Instar Training

An instar performs pattern recognition; that is, it is trained to respond to a specific input vector **X** and to no other. This training is accomplished by adjusting its weights to be like the input vector. The output of the instar is calculated as the weighted sum of its inputs, as described in the preceding paragraphs. Viewed another way, this calculation produces the dot product of the input vector with the weight vector, a measure of similarity for normalized

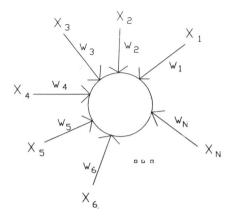

Figure C-1. Grossberg Instar

vectors. Hence, the neuron comes to respond most strongly to the input pattern for which it was trained.

The training operation is expressed in the formula that follows:

$$w_i(t + 1) = w_i(t) + \alpha[x_i - w_i(t)]$$

where
$w_i(t)$ = the weight from input x_i
x_i = the ith input
α = the training rate coefficient, which starts around 0.1 and is gradually reduced during the training process

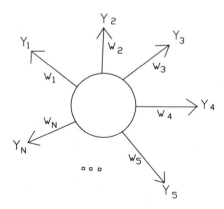

Figure C-2. Grossberg Outstar

When fully trained, application of the input vector **X** will activate the trained instar neuron. It may be observed that this can be accomplished in a single training cycle if α is set to 1. While this is true, it eliminates the ability of the instar to generalize. Properly trained, the instar will respond not only to a single specific vector, but to minor variations of that vector as well. This is accomplished by gradually adjusting the neuron's weights as it is trained over a range of vectors representing normal variations of the desired vector. In this way, weights adjust to average values of the training vectors and the neuron develops the ability to respond to any member of that class.

Outstar Training

Whereas the instar fires whenever a specific input pattern is applied, the outstar has a complementary function; it produces a desired excitation pattern to other neurons whenever it fires.

To train an outstar neuron, its weights are adjusted to be like a desired target vector. The training algorithm can be expressed symbolically as follows:

$$w_i(t + 1) = w_i(t) + \beta \left[y_i - w_i(t) \right]$$

where β is a training rate coefficient that starts near 1 and is gradually reduced to zero during the training sequence. As with the instar, the outstar weights are gradually trained over a set of vectors representing normal variations of the ideal. In this way, the output excitation pattern from the neuron represents a statistical measure of the training set, and can actually converge to the ideal vector when all it has seen are distorted versions.

PERCEPTRON TRAINING

In 1957, Rosenblatt (1959) developed a model that stimulated intense interest. While severely limited in its original form, it has become the basis for many of today's more sophisticated supervised training algorithms. The perceptron is of such importance that all of Chapter 2 is dedicated to its presentation; hence, this treatment is brief, and in a somewhat different format.

The perceptron is a two-layer, nonrecurrent network of the type shown in Figure C-3. It uses a supervised training algorithm; hence, the training set consists of a set of input vectors, each with its desired target vector. Input vector components take on a continuous range of values; target vector components are binary valued (either zero or one). After training, the network accepts a set of continuous inputs and produces the desired binary valued outputs.

Training is accomplished as follows:

1. Randomize all network weights to small numbers.
2. Apply an input training vector **X** and calculate the NET signal from each neuron using the standard formula

$$NET_j = \sum_i x_i w_{ij}$$

3. Apply the threshold activation function to the NET signal from each neuron as follows:

$OUT_j = 1$ if NET_j is greater than threshold θ_j

$OUT_j = 0$ otherwise

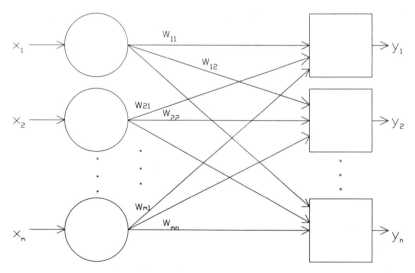

Figure C-3.   A Single-Layer Neural Network

where θ_j is the threshold associated with neuron j. (In the simplest case, all neurons have the same threshold.)

4. Compute the error for each neuron by subtracting the actual output from the target output:

$$\text{error}_j = \text{target}_j - \text{OUT}_j$$

5. Modify each weight as follows:

$$w_{ij}(t + 1) = w_{ij}(t) + \alpha\, x_i\, \text{error}_j$$

6. Repeat steps 2 through 5 until the error is sufficiently low.

WIDROW-HOFF TRAINING

As we have seen, the perceptron was limited to binary outputs. Widrow, along with his graduate student Hoff, extended the perceptron learning algorithm to continuous outputs using the sigmoidal function (Widrow 1959; Widrow and Hoff 1960). In addition, they developed a mathematical proof that the network will eventually converge for any function it is capable of representing. Widrow's first model, the Adeline, had a single-output neuron; his later model, Madeline, extended this to the multi-output case.

The training equations of the Adeline are very similar to those of the perceptron. The critical difference is in step 4, where the continuous NET signal is used rather than the binary-valued OUT. The modified step 4 then reads:

4. Compute the error for each neuron, by subtracting the NET signal from the target output:

$$\text{error}_j = \text{target}_j - \text{NET}_j$$

STATISTICAL TRAINING METHODS

Chapter 5 covers statistical training methods in detail, so only an overview is presented here.

Single-layer networks are severely limited in the problems they can solve, yet for many years no method was known to train multi-layer networks. Statistical training provides a way out of this dilemma, albeit at a substantial cost in computational requirements.

By analogy, training a network by statistical means is like annealing a metal. To anneal a metal, the temperature is first raised until the atoms of the metal move about freely. Then the temperature is gradually reduced, and the atoms continuously seek a minimum energy configuration. At some low temperature, the atoms freeze into the lowest energy configuration possible.

In an artificial neural network, a global measure of network energy is defined as a function of a specified set of network variables. An artificial temperature variable is initialized at a high value, thereby permitting network variables to make large random changes. Changes that result in a reduction in global energy are retained; those that increase energy are retained according to a probability function. The artificial temperature is gradually reduced over time, and the network converges to a global energy minimum.

There are many variations on the statistical training theme. For example, the global energy can be defined as the mean squared error between the actual and desired output vectors of a training set, and the variables can be network weights. In this case, the network can be trained by starting at a high artificial temperature and performing the following steps:

1. Apply a training vector to the input of the network, and calculate the output according to the appropriate network rules.
2. Calculate the mean squared error between the desired and actual output vectors.
3. Change a network weight by a random amount, and then calculate both the new output and the resulting error. If the error is reduced, retain the weight change; otherwise, retain the weight change with a probability determined by the Boltzmann distribution. If not retained, the weight is returned to its previous value.
4. Repeat steps 1 through 3, gradually reducing the artificial temperature.

If the size of the random weight change is selected according to the Boltzmann distribution, convergence to a global minimum is ensured only if the temperature varies inversely as the logarithm of elapsed training time. This may result in intolerably long training sessions, so a great deal of effort has been expended to find faster training methods. By choosing the step size from the Cauchy distribution (as in Szu's Cauchy machine) the temperature may be reduced inversely with training time, thereby yielding a major reduction in the time required for convergence.

Note that there is a class of statistical methods for neural networks in which the network variables are neuron outputs rather than weights. Chapter 5 treats these algorithms in detail.

SELF-ORGANIZATION

Kohonen (1984) has reported interesting and useful results from his research on self-organizing maps used for pattern recognition tasks. In general, these maps classify a pattern represented by a vector of values in which each component of the vector corresponds to an element of the pattern. Kohonen's algorithms are based upon a nonsupervised learning technique. Once trained, application of an input vector from a given class will produce excitation levels in each output neuron; the neuron with the maximum excitation represents the classification. Because the training is performed without a target vector, there is no way to predict prior to training which neuron will be associated with a given class of input vectors. However, this mapping is easily done by testing the network after it is trained.

The algorithm treats the set of n weights entering a neuron as a vector in n-dimensional space. Prior to training, each component of this weight vector is initialized to random values. Then each vector is normalized to make it of unit length in weight space. This is done by dividing each random weight by the square root of the sum of the squares of the components of that weight vector.

All of the input vectors in the training set are likewise normalized to unit length, and the network is trained according to the algorithm that follows:

1. Apply an input vector **X**.
2. Calculate the distance D_j (in n dimensional space) between **X** and the weight vectors **W**$_j$ of each neuron. In Euclidean space, this is calculated as follows:

$$\mathbf{D}_j = \sqrt{\left[\sum_i (x_i - w_{ij})^2 \right]}$$

where
    x_i = component i of input vector **X**
    w_{ij} = the weight from input i to neuron j

3. The neuron that has the weight vector closest to **X** is declared the winner. This weight vector, called **W**$_c$, becomes the center of a group of weight vectors that lie within a distance D from **W**$_c$.
4. Train this group of nearby weight vectors according to the formula that follows:

$$\mathbf{W}_j(t + 1) = \mathbf{W}_j(t) + \alpha[\mathbf{X} - \mathbf{W}_j(t)] \text{ for all weight vectors}$$
$$\text{within a distance } D \text{ of } \mathbf{W}_c$$

5. Perform steps 1 through 4, cycling through each input vector.

As the network trains, gradually reduce the values of D and α. Kohonen recommends that α should start near 1 and go down to 0.1, whereas D can start out as large as the greatest distance between weight vectors, and end up so small that only one neuron is trained.

Up to a point, the classification accuracy will improve with additional training. Kohonen recommends that the number of training cycles should be at least 500 times the number of output neurons for good statistical accuracy.

The training algorithm adjusts the weight vectors in the vicinity of the winning neuron to be more like the input vector. Because all vectors are normalized to unit length, they may be considered to be points on a unit hypersphere. The training operation then moves the cluster of nearby weight points so that they are closer to the input vector point.

It is assumed that the input vectors are actually clustered into classes that are similar, hence, close in vector space. A specific class will tend to control a specific neuron, rotating its weight vector toward the center of the class, making it more likely to be the winner when any member of that class is applied to the input.

After training, classification is performed by applying an arbitrary vector, calculating the excitation produced for each neuron, and then selecting the neuron with the highest excitation as the indicator of the correct classification.

References

Grossberg, S. 1974. Classical and instrumental learning by neural networks. *Progress in theoretical biology*, vol. 3, pp. 51–141. New York: Academic Press.

Hebb, D. O., 1949. *Organization of behavior*. New York: Science Editions.

Kohonen, T. 1984. *Self-organization and associative memory*, Series in Information Sciences, vol. 8. Berlin: Springer Verlag.

Rosenblatt, R. 1959. *Principles of neurodynamics*. New York: Spartan Books.

Widrow, B. 1959. Adaptive sampled-data systems, a statistical theory of adaptation. *1959 IRE WESCON Convention Record*, part 4. New York: Institute of Radio Engineers.

Widrow, B., and Hoff, M. 1960. Adaptive switching circuits. *1960 IRE WESCON Convention Record*. New York: Institute of Radio Engineers.

Index